SALT BLOCK

GRILLING

OTHER BOOKS BY MARK BITTERMAN

Salted: A Manifesto on the World's Most Essential Mineral, with Recipes

Salt Block Cooking: 70 Recipes for Grilling, Chilling, Searing, and Serving on Himalayan Salt Blocks

Bitterman's Field Guide to Bitters & Amari: 500 Bitters; 50 Amari; 123 Recipes for Cocktails, Food & Homemade Bitters

Bitterman's Craft Salt Cooking: The Single Ingredient That Transforms All Your Favorite Foods and Recipes

SALT BLOCK
GRILLING

70 Recipes for Outdoor Cooking with Himalayan Salt Blocks

MARK BITTERMAN

Recipes by Andrew Schloss and Mark Bitterman
Photography by Aubrie LeGault and Mark Bitterman

Andrews McMeel
Publishing®

a division of Andrews McMeel Universal

To my sister, Jenny

CONTENTS

INTRODUCTION

THE ORIGIN OF SALT BLOCK GRILLING

Grilling conjures different images—our past expressed in snapshots of the great times we all spend outdoors. Near a sandy beach, paper plates and condiments strewn across a picnic blanket, ice chests stocked with burger patties and potato salad, and dogs run up from the water shaking their wet fur over everyone. In the wooded mountains, a tin coffeepot steaming on a rock at the edge of a fire pit, kids giggling in the tent, and trout and eggs frying in butter. In the hills of Tuscany, a cold, bitter drink gathering droplets of condensation on the table, the gregarious chef explaining in Italian (which you don't understand) the finer points of slow-grilling pork shoulder and wild herbs. In your backyard, neighbors arrive with a six-pack of their latest home brew, lured by thick steaks, onions, and asparagus marinating while the coals slowly catch and glow. Cooking fresh foods over fire connects us to the pleasure of today and the anticipation of days to come like nothing else. Salt blocks are the next adventure in grilling, a new way to bring the best memories of the past into the future.

The discovery of salt block grilling is threefold: Thick blocks of scorching hot salt bring fantastically effective new techniques to the grill, including convection cooking, searing, simultaneously grilling from below and searing from above, and even cooking from within the food itself. Food gets cooked better,

faster, and more perfectly. Salt blocks drive flavor in cooking like nothing else, enlisting the dynamic duo of salt and fire in a single smoldering slab. Salt draws moisture so the heat can brown and crisp the food even as the salt and fire join forces on another front, breaking down both proteins and starches to create texture and flavor. Those objective benefits aside, the greatest promise of salt blocks is surely the newfound sense of adventure they bring to meals prepared under the banner of a blue sky. Salt blocks revive the excitement of familiar places, take you to new ones, and expand the realm of what's possible in outdoor cooking.

Himalayan salt blocks are made of solid salt, formed 600 million years ago when salt deposits from an evaporated sea were buried deep under the earth. Geologists call this natural mineral *salt halite*. Giant boulders of it, sometimes in excess of 500 pounds, are extracted from ancient mines in the Salt Range of Pakistan's Punjab region. The boulders are then sliced and diced into innumerable shapes and sizes using stone-cutting saws and lathes. Miners, obsessed with stone and all its permutable charms, have long fashioned objects from boulders of salt, or even carved reliefs directly into the walls of the mine. The biggest of these salt mines in Pakistan is the Khewra mine, which features a veritable theme park of salt-hewn sights, including replicas of famous mosques and the Great Wall of China.

By far the most common use for Himalayan salt is to grind it into cooking salt. Unlike industrially made salts like kosher salt and iodized table salt, Himalayan salt contains over eighty trace elements. Where refined salts taste harsh and acrid, this salt tastes rich and balanced. This rich flavor shines through on foods cooked on Himalayan Salt Blocks.

Contrary to all the marketing and hype, Himalayan salt blocks are not actually from the Himalayas. In fact, there are few if any salt mines in the Himalayas. The name was introduced by marketing-savvy folks in the health food industry in the 1970s and '80s, and it has proven impossible to shake the term ever since, though few have tried. When I first began selling Himalayan salt in my shop, The Meadow, back in 2006, I tried to popularize the name Punjabi Pink, but people would look right past it and say they were only interested in the "pink salt from Tibet," or, my favorite, "pink sea salt from the Himalayas," which posited not only an imaginary salt mine in the Himalayas, but also an entire imaginary sea. So with apologies to the excellent people who live and work in Punjab, we will continue to call their pink salt *Himalayan*.

The good people of Pakistan, as well as those of neighboring India, who buy enormous quantities of Pakistan's prized pink salt, do not cook on salt blocks. With mind-bogglingly rich culinary traditions of their own, they cannot be blamed for their lack of innovation on this front. It was in America—where fresh meat and produce and a blazing bed of coals equals cuisine—that salt block grilling first took off. My previous book, *Salt Block Cooking,* remains the standard reference for serving, curing, warming, melting, baking, freezing, and even drinking with blocks, bowls, and cups of Himalayan salt. *Salt Block Grilling* is the first book dedicated solely to the perfect marriage of salt blocks and the grill.

A SALT BLOCK FOR EVERY GRILL

Himalayan salt blocks have settled onto most of the surfaces of my kitchen, and I use them daily. I keep the butter out by the stove on a four-inch-thick cube of salt that keeps the butter cool and fresh (remember that salt is a preservative) even when the stove gets hot. Appetizers like radishes and butter, fruit and cheese, and olives and meats are almost always served on a salt block, as are many salads, whether it's avocados and jicama, tomatoes and mozzarella, cucumbers and onions, or pears and endive. I cook on salt bocks whenever the food warrants it; scallops, duck breast, or shrimp in their shells simply don't compare when cooked in a pan. If I'm having guests over, I use salt blocks more deliberately, because their primordial beauty contributes to the atmosphere of hospitality and chitchat. I'll even serve mint juleps or oyster shooters in little shot glasses that have been lathed by hand out of salt blocks. But for all of a salt block's utility and appeal in the kitchen, it is in the great outdoors where they really shine.

So how does a salt block make the world a better place? Let me count the ways:

1. A salt block is heavy. Anything you put under it will be smashed flat. Put a halved chicken on the grill and a salt block on top of it, and you get a smashed-flat halved chicken, which means ruffled ridges of crispy skin where it was pressed against the grate, plus firmer flesh and quicker, more even cooking.

2. Salt blocks have huge thermal mass. Ye olde cast-iron skillet is like tinfoil by comparison. This thermal mass evens out the cooking temperature of whatever you put on top of it, so food burns less, sears better, and is, overall, more flawlessly executed.

3. Salt blocks have huge thermal mass, Part II. Pizza stones, oven bricks, diffusers, and all manner of things have been created to generate the massive blast of heat that so many foods crave, from naan dough to diver scallops. Salt blocks deliver tremendously even heat– three times that of a pizza stone.

4. Moisture from food quickly dissolves a micro-layer of the salt block, and this salty water quickly evaporates to form a salty crust on the surface of the food. The words *salty crust* are synonymous with the words *hot dang* when it comes to grilled foods.

5. The amount of salt that a food picks up is a function of the food's moisture and the heat of the salt block, so by controlling either or both you can dial exactly the amount of flavor you want into a food. Fatty foods like a fillet

of salmon can be grilled at superhot temperatures for the ultimate crispy skin. Sweet foods like cookies can be cooked at a much lower temperature to coax gentle saltiness into the mix—and at the same time, the hot block gently browns the sugar in the dough to create insane salted-caramel flavor.

6. Salt blocks give you a new, solid work surface on the grill, a place to sear vegetables or shrimp or sausage that might otherwise fall between the grates.

7. Salt blocks can be used to bring the good times back indoors. If it's chilly out, start out on the grill, then move the white-hot salt block to a ceramic trivet indoors and finish cooking at the table. Try doing this with a hibachi.

8. Salt blocks are versatile. You can use the same block for scallops one day and steak the next, and duck breast the next and eggs after that. Unless the dish is something intensely oily and fragrant, like salt-seared fresh sardines, the salt will not carry over flavors of the preceding meal into the next.

9. Before you ever use your salt block on the grill, try it as a serving platter. Fruits,

vegetables, cheeses, and more will pick up a faint saltiness from the block. The block will grow pale and opaque, losing some of its dazzling translucent pink beauty once it is heated, so seize the opportunity to serve a meal or two on your new salt block before you grill on it the first time.

10. Salt blocks dress and impress. With a heavy-duty pot holder or a metal rack, you can serve your food on the same salt block that grilled it. Give your guests something to talk about.

11. Salt block grilling is new and it's taking the grilling world by storm. This means that now is the time to get down the fundamentals, figure out a few tricks of your own, and be a part of great things to come.

This book is broken into six chapters: Meat, Poultry, Seafood, Vegetables and Fruit, Dairy, and Dough. As might be expected in a book about grilling, most dishes are savory, such as Salt Block Tandoori Chicken (page 87), Salt-Seared Baby Octopus with Sesame Leaf Salad and Yuzu Dressing (page 93), or Salt-Roasted Pork Loin with Juniper Crust (page 50).

Some wonderful opportunities to make sweets are also explored. Flatbreads, cookies,

and biscuits bake beautifully on a salt block set over a moderate fire on a closed grill. Salty-Smoky Walnut-Chocolate-Chunk-Cookies (page 160) are a must-try, as are Salt-Block-Baked Smoked-Cheese Scones with Chipotle Honey (page 172). Looking beyond doughs, try Salt-Stoned Bananas Foster with Rye Whisky Caramel (page 139) or Maple-Drenched Salt-Seared Pig Candy (page 55). In addition to traditionally formatted recipes, you will find a specific recipe table in each chapter. These tables offer up variations on a master salt-block-grilling technique and then leverage them to create recipes for many different concepts, cuisines, and ingredients.

KNOW THY SALT BLOCK

Your Himalayan salt block will take on a life of its own once you start grilling with it. While it might be nice for salt to offer all the indestructability of stainless steel, this is simply not the case. When heated, it will change color dramatically and may develop fissures or even large cracks. It may also patina with use, taking on color from the proteins cooked on it. But don't worry, salt is a complicated, wily, unpredictable substance. This is what gives it much of its charm and its unique culinary advantages.

The more stable a cooking vessel is, the less it interacts with the food cooked in it. Because metals are mostly toxic, material stability is a distinct advantage when evaluating one type of metal cookware over another. But when your cookware is made from salt, playing with the interaction between food and cooking surface becomes a big part of the culinary art.

Himalayan salt can range in color from perfectly clear to amber yellow; from pearly pink to feisty, meaty red; and from steel gray to the silver-blue of Waterford crystal. The colors are allopathic, meaning they come from various trace minerals trapped in the salt crystal matrix: iron, magnesium, copper, potassium, and dozens of others. Every mineral in the earth's crust, and in your body, has a role in the cast of characters.

SALT BLOCK PHYSICS

Here's a quick look at the basic physics of how a salt block and its salt work together with our food. Salt blocks naturally bring a world of tangy saltiness to your food. It is your job to harness nature's will and bend it to your own. Master the five basic physical principles behind cooking on salt blocks and you will get great results every time.

1. Moisture—wetter foods take on more salt faster
2. Time—the longer a food cooks on a salt block, the more salt it takes in
3. Temperature—searing food on very hot salt blocks reduces the amount of salt it absorbs
4. Fat—fat on a salt block reduces the amount of salt interacting with the surface of the food
5. Thickness—thick and dense food can interact longer with salt on its surface without becoming too salty

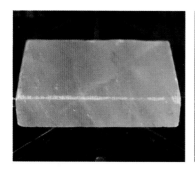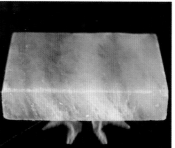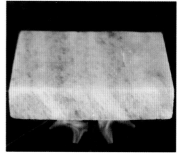

Himalayan salt blocks have very little porosity, which keeps food from sticking to their surface, and virtually no residual moisture (.026 percent), allowing salt blocks to be safely heated or chilled to great extremes. Himalayan pink salt blocks have a high specific heat capacity that makes heavy-gauge premium metal cookware seem like tinfoil by comparison.

We have tested salt blocks from -321°F up to 900°F (-196°C to 482°C), freezing them with liquid nitrogen to make crazy cool ice and blasting them on the hottest coal fire to make crackling good flatbread. Salt won't melt until it reaches 1473.4°F (800.8°C), so you have a huge temperature range with which to experiment.

Two other considerations come into play when working with Himalayan salt plates. It's counterintuitive, but a huge flat block of salt actually delivers salt to food in a very modest, deliberate, and measured way. A salt block's lack of porosity means that it has only one flat surface to offer food, compared to the multitudes of facets in a crystal of granular salt. Because a salt block has only one solid surface that's in contact with your food, it dissolves slowly and imparts its seasoning in a moderate way. Second, the high quantity of trace minerals (1.2 percent sulfur, .4 percent calcium, .35 percent potassium, .16 percent magnesium, and 80 other trace minerals) mitigates the full-frontal saltiness of pure sodium chloride, so the actual flavor of the salt that the block imparts is more balanced, and, by extension, it elicits more complex flavors from your food.

While a block needs to be at least 1½ inches thick for stovetop cooking (and 2 inches is even better), grills heat with such uniformity that thinner blocks can work, provided they are absolutely top quality.

BLOCK SHOPPING

The better quality the salt block, the longer it will last and the less likely something will go wrong, such as breaking or even exploding. The best way to ensure quality is to buy your salt block from a trusted brand or from a dealer who has excellent contacts at the source. Pay a little extra; the best-quality salt costs more. There are many people producing salt blocks in Pakistan, but most of them deal in inferior grades of salt, either because it is far more economical or because they don't know any better. Ideally, buy from a retailer that provides guarantees against breakage. Avoid going for the cheapest block from an anonymous retailer who has no written guarantee.

Before shopping, decide what you want to use your salt block for. Some vendors now differentiate the quality of the blocks according to their end use. At my shops, we grade our blocks into categories: blocks suitable for cookware for heating; blocks used at room temperature for serving; and irregularly formed blocks that are aesthetically stunning but would not be suitable for heating. We even sell "architectural" blocks for construction of things like walls in spas and restaurants, light sculptures, and "meat lockers" for dry aging.

You can find my own brand of salt blocks at bittermansalt.com or at Sur La Table stores.

Select blocks that appear smooth and plain. Although veins and variations in color are dramatic looking, they sometimes indicate planes on which the block is apt to crack. Blocks for grilling should have minimal deep cracks, and any strata of color should be soft rather than clearly defined. Ideally, the block should be consistently translucent (not transparent), but opaque blocks can work well, too. Avoid any block that has lots of loose, "crunchy-looking" crystal facets throughout. These blocks can be the most beautiful for serving uses, but the facets harbor moisture. The moisture will vaporize when heated, causing the block to break or even pop like a giant piece of halite popcorn. Make sure you buy from someone who knows his or her salt.

SALT BLOCK SIZES

Many people's first instinct is to buy a huge slab of salt for grilling. Before you purchase one, think about the types of foods you plan to cook on it. Larger and heavier salt blocks are generally good. The most versatile size for grilling two to four entrée-size portions is a (8 to 10-inch) square, but the most economical option is to purchase two or more 4 x 8 x 2-inch salt bricks and use them to pave your grill grate.

One advantage of 4 x 8 x 2-inch bricks of salt is that smaller blocks are easier to handle and clean. Another advantage is that because they are smaller, they are less prone to break, and if they do break, you can simply replace the broken brick with a new one rather than having to purchase a whole new larger one. Also, the larger salt blocks often cost considerably more than the equivalent size made up of several smaller salt blocks.

The other advantage to paving is the increased flexibility. When you have many brick-sized blocks, you can custom pave the area of your grill according to the needs of each meal. Sometimes I'll pave just a corner of the grill and light the fire going under the block side of the grill only. Then I can sear off some chicken on the salt block and then finish it on the exposed part of the grill grate, where it cooks indirectly from the connecting currents trapped under the hood of the grill. Other times, such as at a big barbecue, I'll pave the entire grill from end to end and sear up a mess of shrimp and skirt steak.

Paving isn't perfect, of course. You do have to be cognizant of the cracks between blocks when putting food on them, but I find that the advantages outweigh the inconvenience.

ESSENTIAL UTENSILS

There are several tools that will make salt block grilling not only easier, but also safer. Infrared laser thermometers are helpful for gauging the temperature of salt blocks. Aim these little gun-shaped lasers at a nonreflective surface; pull the trigger and get an accurate temperature reading. Once very expensive, laser thermometers have become very affordable. Most cooks get a pretty good sense of the temperature of a salt block by spattering a little water on it and observing how rapidly it evaporates off (see Getting It Hot, page 18). A laser thermometer should be rated to measure up to 700°F. Some also measure cool temperatures to -50°F or lower.

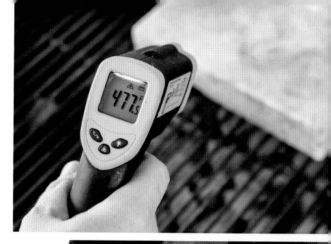

Heavy, professional-grade oven or grill mitts are indispensable. A salt block on a barbecue grill is bulky, awkward, very heavy, and potentially very, very hot. Hands will be right over the heat source when adjusting its position or holding it in place to flip or remove food. Moving the block means lifting it from the bottom, right where the heat source was heating it! Oven mitts must provide the following: (1) solid protection against heat for at least one minute; (2) resistance to temperatures up to 800°F; (3) flame retardation, especially if lifting the block from a lit grill; and (4) good grip.

Consumer-grade oven mitts are generally not up to this task. Silicone mitts melt at around 500°F, and cotton and wool ones burn or singe at around 600°F. Rather than spend a fortune at hardware or restaurant supply stores, visit a local welding supply store, where you can choose from a solid selection of very heavy-duty gloves. I go for puppet-style mitts or gloves with fire-retardant Nomex uppers and sleeves. Amazingly, for about $20 you can get a pair of top-quality gloves that do a proper job of helping to keep your hands out of harm's way.

A good stainless steel spatula with a long handle is the essential implement for grilling on a salt block. Salt is not a nonstick surface. Turning or removing the food with a rubber, wood, or Teflon spatula will likely leave that most beautiful of beautiful layers of browned and salted delectableness on the block. To flip or remove food, hold the salt block steady with a thick oven mitt or grill mitt, and then press down very firmly, scraping hard along the surface of the salt block. Don't be afraid to put some muscle into it!

Trivets are another essential for cooking on or serving from hot salt blocks at the table. Ceramic is an excellent insulator and can withstand very high temperatures. Do not use trivets made of silicone or wood, as they will melt or burn, ruining your salt block, your trivet, or both. Whatever you do, do not use a metal trivet! Metal will resist the heat just fine, but it will also conduct all that energy from the salt block right onto your table! This will almost certainly ruin your table—not to mention the real tragedy of also draining heat from the block so rapidly that it will not do its job cooking the food. The ideal materials are highly heat-resistant ones with low thermal conductivity, such as ceramic. My preferred setup is a solid ceramic trivet with a silicone trivet beneath that to provide added thermal insulation and resistance to slippage.

CARE AND HANDLING

Before cooking with a salt block the first time, give it a quick clean. Salt is inherently sanitary (it is a natural disinfectant), but passing it quickly under cold water removes any dust or debris. Wipe with a clean cloth to dry. Paper towels work OK, but any rough bits on the surface of the block may catch and shred the paper, leaving a little confetti behind. Another benefit of rinsing the block is that it dissolves some of the bits of salt flaked up during manufacturing and transportation, burnishing it to its naturally lush, resonant color.

The top surface of a salt block can be heated to over 600°F, but the bottom will get even hotter—in excess of 900°F. Because unlike a skillet, salt blocks don't have handles; you should always use very heavy fire-resistant oven mitts when handling them.

Note that salt blocks hold more than ten times as much energy as a pot, so anything you set them on after being removed from the fire will be subject to intense heat. A hot block can easily scorch your table, your counter, or you. Before moving a hot salt block, prepare a place to put it, such as a trivet (see page 15) or a spot on your range, turn off the heat source before moving the block (if possible) to reduce the risk of scorching your oven mitts, and alert others around you that you are coming through with a hot salt block in your hands.

A great trick to make cleaning your block easier is to turn off the heat, or remove the salt block from the hot grill, a few minutes before the food is done cooking. The block will continue to cook the food for some minutes at virtually the same temperature, as the energy from the bottom of the block continues to conduct through the block, so cooking will not be affected. The advantage is that the block will start cooling down just enough so that when the food is removed, it will have much less energy with which to carbonize any food adhering to the block. Not only will this make the block much easier to clean, but it will also help preserve its natural good looks by reducing the patina that comes from too much burned-on food.

On a related note, turning the heat to low for two or three minutes rather than completely off slows down the rate of cooling, minimizing the thermal stresses. While I have never had a problem with a block breaking due to cooling too fast, there is an audible difference in the fewer crackling sounds coming from the block, indicating that the crystals are experiencing less stress and developing fewer fissures.

GETTING IT HOT A salt block's warm-up rate depends on the amount of energy put into it and the mass of the block. Before heating your salt block for the first time, please read the sidebar on page 21 ("Read This Before Heating a Salt Block!") for important cautions and disclaimers.

Larger blocks take longer to heat than smaller ones, and weaker heat sources need more time than more powerful ones.

In addition, there are some basic physics to consider.

A nice, expensive 10-inch aluminum-core stainless steel fry pan weighs about 2.5 pounds and has about 200 square inches of surface area with the rim. A 10-inch-diameter, 1.5-inch-thick salt block has about the same surface area but it weighs 12 pounds. This additional mass takes more energy and time to heat and to cool.

In addition, every pound of salt stores 2 kilojoules of energy versus well under 1 kilojoule of energy stored by the pan. The pan heats and cools rapidly because it only holds a small amount of energy and because the aluminum in it conducts heat incredibly well. The salt block can contain approximately ten times the amount of energy. On top of that, the salt is not very conductive, so energy is slow to travel through it.

Patience is essential, and the process is so different from preheating an oven, a skillet, or a pot of pasta water that you should consider adopting the habit of using a clock or timer to keep track, at least until you get the hang of it.

HEATING STEP BY STEP

Heat your salt block slowly, especially the first time you use it. Heating in three stages gives the crystal lattice of the salt block time to expand slowly, minimizing stresses that could cause a block to crack.

STEP 1: VERY LOW: Place the block over the low flame of a gas grill or next to a low-to-moderate-heat bed of coals. Heat for 15 minutes.

STEP 2: MEDIUM: Increase the flame of a gas grill to medium, or for a charcoal grill, move the block directly over the low-to-moderate bed of coals. Heat for 15 minutes.

STEP 3: HIGH: Increase the flame to high on a gas grill, or for charcoal, stoke the fire with fresh coals to heat the block over high heat for 15 minutes.

The duration of the last stage can be shortened or lengthened depending on the final temperature desired: five to seven minutes for cooler temperatures in the 400°F to 450°F range, eight to twelve minutes for temperatures in the 450°F to 500°F range, and twelve to twenty minutes for temperatures in the 500°F to 550°F range or higher.

HEATING 101

Salt crystals expand when heated. This means your salt block will expand when put on the grill. Because salt blocks are thick and slow to transmit heat, so the temperature difference between the bottom of the block and the top of the block can be extreme. In addition, grills do not always throw off the most uniform heat. The upshot is that different areas of the block will be subject to different rates of thermal expansion as it heats. The resulting different rates of thermal expansion put stress on the block. There may also be small amounts of moisture hiding in tiny fissures within the salt itself, accumulated along the road from the womb of the mountains in Pakistan to your kitchen counter. When heated, the water will convert to steam.

Giving your salt block plenty of time to warm from room temperature to 150°F or 200°F gives any moisture locked in the matrix of the crystals time to escape and allows the heat to spread evenly through the block, minimizing the stresses caused by expansion. As the block heats, microfissures form in the more or less monolithic salt crystals, turning the block from translucent pink to an opaque pinkish-white. This "tempering" of the salt block greatly increases its durability, and it will be far less likely to crack during heating in future uses.

READ THIS BEFORE HEATING A SALT BLOCK!

A salt block is a natural stone that requires special treatment. Over the years I have grown to be both very casual and very intuitive about using salt blocks. The gist of it is that it's easy and routine. However, there are risks, and special consideration should be given, especially the first time you use one.

- Salt blocks can crack. Heat them slowly.
- Salt blocks can pop. Only use cookware-graded blocks.
- Salt blocks get very hot. If you must handle them, handle them only very briefly, using extreme caution, professional high-temperature oven mitts (see page 15), or a salt block holder.
- Salt blocks hold enormous energy. When using a hot salt block away from the grill, ensure adequate insulation between the block and tables and counters.

Depending on how hot you need to get your block, most of the time you will start heating it before you even begin assembling ingredients for your dish. Between thirty minutes and an hour before you are ready to start grilling, put the salt block(s) on an unheated gas grill. Heat the grill to low, cover the grill, and warm the block for 15 minutes. Once the block is tempered, raise the heat to medium, and wait another 15 minutes. Raise it to high, and wait another 15 minutes, then check the temperature.

If you are using charcoal, bank a chimney of red-hot charcoal briquettes to one side of the firebox. Put the block on the grill grate away from the fire, and cover the grill. In fifteen minutes add more pieces of charcoal to the fire and, using grill gloves, move the block so that it is over the new coals. Because the coals ignite and heat slowly, there is no need for the third step mentioned above; in thirty minutes or so your block will be ready for grilling.

Infrared laser thermometers are a great tool for gauging the precise temperature of a salt block (see page 14), but anyone familiar with heating a skillet will get the hang of it pretty quickly. A laser thermometer aimed at the center of the block will tell you that you have reached your target temperature.

A rough estimate of temperature can also be gleaned by spattering a small amount of water on the surface: At 300°F, the water will boil off in two to five seconds; at 400°F, it will sizzle off in one or two seconds; and at 500°F, it will hardly touch the surface before skating off and vanishing in its own vapor. I use my hand to gauge temperature. If I bring it down slowly over the block and self-preservation kicks in when it is about an inch above the surface, I know the block is at around 525°F.

TABLETOP SALT BLOCK COOKING

Salt blocks retain heat beautifully. This is an invitation to use them not just on the grill, but on the table as well. Hot salt blocks can be pulled from the grill and transferred to the table, where food can continue to be seared.

Put a regular hot pad or silicone pot holder on the table, and place a ceramic trivet atop that. The ceramic is both fireproof and easily resists the 900°F temperatures at the underside of a salt block that has been on the grill. The block will retain enough heat for two or three rounds of quick-seared foods.

Alternatively, for more protracted tabletop salt block cooking, use a small propane caterer's stove. They cost about $20 and can be used for all manner of cooking, with or without salt blocks.

CLEANING

Allow the block to cool fully to room temperature before cleaning, at least three or four hours. Moisten the salt block by wiping it with a wet sponge, then scrub vigorously with a steel scouring pad

(a green scrubby will also work) at any areas where food has stuck, and wipe away any loosened pieces with a damp sponge. Do not use a soap-infused pad like S.O.S. or Brillo, as the soap will penetrate into the block and ruin it. Repeat the process until the surface is clean, then pat dry (do not wipe or rub) with a clean rag or paper towel. Let stand at room temperature for a few hours more to evaporate off any remaining moisture.

Note that no salt block will ever return fully to its preheated splendor. They will turn an opaque, pale white-pink. It is OK to clean off any adhering food, but don't obsess on scrubbing it all the way down to a pristine state. Like a cast-iron skillet, salt blocks should take on a natural patina from the foods cooked on them. Excessive cleaning will shorten the life of a block.

STORAGE
Salt blocks are hygroscopic (water attracting). They will suck moisture out of the air, so store the block in a place where humidity is at a minimum. Unless you live in the 100 percent humidity of a Borneo jungle, you can probably leave your salt block on the counter or in a cupboard alongside other dishes. Even though I live in the wet

and rainy climes of the Pacific Northwest, my salt blocks do just fine scattered around the house wherever I happen to find a place for them. If you do live in a humid place and your salt block is always damp (and maybe even tends to collect water), you can wrap it in a few layers of paper towels and seal it in a zipper-lock plastic bag to keep it from absorbing atmospheric moisture. Some people choose to keep their salt blocks in the refrigerator, where humidity is consistently low due to the simple fact that cold air holds less moisture than warm air. This does work OK, and makes it so you always have a chilled salt block at the ready, but it does take up valuable refrigerator space.

DEATH AND REBIRTH OF A SALT BLOCK

How do you know if your salt block is kaput? Old salt blocks don't die; they just crumble away. A well-maintained, high-quality cookware block may last for dozens of uses, but salt blocks do eventually break. If they do, feel free to keep using them anyway. So long as the block presents a useful surface, you can continue to serve or cook with it. Even small rocks of salt or broken-up salt blocks can be used for roasting Orange-Rosemary Game Hens (page 71), or Honey Hot Pepper Roast Chicken (page 71).

The end of a block's utility as a cooking surface spells the beginning of its utility as a cooking salt. It is still natural, good salt. Even blocks that have been cooked on extensively can still be used broken up and tossed in a skillet as a hot bed for cooking meats, fish, and root vegetables.

Salt blocks bring new freedom to grilling—freedom to cook what you want, the way it wants to be cooked. This means more creativity, more fun, and better results. The following recipes explore and illustrate some of their many formidable benefits. Salt blocks disperse heat more gradually and uniformly than an open flame—a boon for difficult-to-grill vegetables, like beets and potatoes, and for baking such as the Salty-Smoky Walnut-Chocolate-Chunk Cookies (page 160). Because salt blocks retain heat longer than any other cookware, they can be used for cooking after they come off the flame in Salt-Seared Watermelon Salad (page 123), for keeping food warm at the table in Raclette (page 146), or as an alternate heat source for grilling thinly sliced meats from above and below at the same time in Atlas Clucked (page 66) and Salt-Seared Chicken Paillards

with Balsamic-Sage Butter (page 72). They are the only pieces of cooking equipment that season as they sear, and at 600 million documented years, salt blocks are bound to have the deepest provenance of anything you own. If you are someone who gets psyched about abandoning the civilized constraints of your indoor kitchen for the adventure of making dinner over an uncalibrated flame under a star-flecked sky, then upping the ante by adding a slab of prehistoric salt just might make your quest that much more incendiary.

CHAPTER 1
MEAT

Evidence of mankind's use of fire dates back to the Early Stone Age, perhaps more than a million years ago, and its use had likely become common as far back as 350,000 years. Since modern humans didn't appear on the scene until about 200,000 years ago, we must concede the invention of fire to our predecessors, *Homo erectus*. Fire tenderizes meat, develops flavor, and provides some protection against spoilage, so it is almost certain that among the first things ever done with fire was to cook meat. In fact, some scientists point to our relatively dull teeth and weak jaws as evidence that cooked meat is what gave rise to our species. We have been doing it for millennia. So what happens when you throw a hot block of salt into the mix?

The richly marbled protein of beef and pork, lovingly salted, is naturally enhanced by exposure to flame. The surface chars and browns, the interior fat melts, and any chunks of salt on the outside of your steaks and chops commingle with concentrating juices on the surface to form a crust that contrasts deliciously with the relatively untouched, unseasoned succulence inside. The salt and the heat both work in their own ways to unravel and break up proteins, creating more flavor available amino acids, so their united efforts don't simply enhance flavor, they create it. Adding a hot salt block between fire and meat doesn't alter this alchemy as much as it enhances it. The surface of the meat releases just enough moisture to dissolve some of the salt, which aids in drawing out just a little more moisture as the heat of the block sears it to a beautiful crust. The differences are both minimal and profound: less char, more flavor. Salt blocks also take out a lot of the guesswork inherent in cooking over an open flame, which definitely has a life of its own.

To make the most of your salt block, it is important to match its temperature to the cut of meat you're cooking. Tender or thin cuts, like fillets, steaks, or pork medallions, need a superhot block, at least 550°F, to sear the surface without overcooking the center. Burgers call for more moderate temperatures, 400°F to 450°F. You will notice that we crank the heat up initially in our master burger recipe for Bacon Browned Pork Belly Burgers (page 45). However, by grilling the condiments first—onion, mushrooms, etc.—the surface temperature of the block is brought down so that it will be perfect to brown the burger without burning the surface. Sometimes we keep the heat high and compensate for the high heat by prepping the meat for a superquick grill time. We slice large cuts like sirloin steak into small pieces and flash sear them in recipes similar to the Lamb Satay with Mint Chutney and Spicy Peanut Crumble (page 59), or transform other tough cuts like short rib into taco meat in Short Rib Tacos (page 43) or kebabs in the Anticuchos with Chile Morita Salsa (page 40) and cook them only slightly longer.

Grilling meats on salt blocks feeds our lust for adventure and satisfies our need for control, but, most importantly, it brings flavor to every food it touches. We can only wonder, what if *Homo erectus* had thought to take it one step further, and grilled with salt blocks instead of simple fire? Imagine what we might have evolved to today.

SANDWICH STEAK CHOPPED ON A SALT BLOCK WITH PEPPERS, ONIONS, AND AGED PROVOLONE

Philadelphia's famous cheesy chopped-steak sandwiches may not be the best food the city has to offer (I've had tremendous Italian, Uzbek, Cambodian, and soul food there), but I like to think this iconic sandwich is a true reflection of a noble class spirit. Sad thing is, cheesesteaks are an endangered species now, and many of my favorite joints have closed up shop for good. Salt-seared vegetables chopped into juicy steak and melded together under zesty provolone tastes like a daydream of times gone by, when a good sandwich was all anyone needed in the City of Brotherly Love.

1 (8 to 10-inch) square salt block, at least 1½ inches thick

2 garlic cloves, minced

Leaves from 8 thyme sprigs

Leaves from 6 oregano sprigs

Leaves from 4 stems of basil, finely chopped

½ cup olive oil

Freshly ground black pepper

4 (6-inch) steak rolls, split

1 large red bell pepper, stemmed, seeded, and cut into thin strips

½ red onion, halved, thinly sliced, and broken into strips

4 ounces white mushrooms, sliced

1 pound boneless beef top round, shaved for steak sandwiches

12 slices provolone cheese, about 8 ounces total

An hour before you are ready to start grilling, put the salt block on one side of an unheated gas grill. Heat the grill to low, cover the grill, and warm the block for 20 minutes. Raise the heat under the block to medium and wait another 20 minutes. Raise it to high and wait another 20 minutes. A laser thermometer aimed at the center of the block should register around 550°F. If using charcoal, bank a chimney's worth of red-hot charcoal briquettes to one side of the firebox. Put the block on the grill grate away from the fire and cover the grill. In 20 minutes, add a dozen more pieces of charcoal to the fire and, using grill gloves, move the block so that it is over the new coals. In 30 minutes, your block will be 550°F and ready for grilling.

Meanwhile combine the garlic, herbs, olive oil, and pepper in a medium bowl. Brush the interior of the rolls with a thin film of the oil mixture; set aside.

Toss the bell pepper, onion, and mushrooms with half of the remaining oil mixture. Toss the beef with the rest of the oil mixture. Set both aside.

Dump the vegetables and their oil onto the hot salt block and cook until the vegetables are barely tender, turning them with a thin-blade slotted spatula frequently, about 3 minutes. Remove to a bowl.

Close the grill and allow the block to regain temperature, about 5 minutes.

Put the steak on the hot blocks and cook until it loses its raw look, about 3 minutes, chopping it with a spatula to help it cook evenly. Divide the steak into 4 piles; top each pile with 3 slices of cheese. Close the grill and cook until the cheese melts, about 30 seconds. Using a spatula, fill each roll with one of the piles of cheesesteak. Top with a portion of the vegetables and serve immediately.

SCOTCHED T-BONE WITH STILTON-POBLANO BUTTER

The T of a T-bone separates two desirable cuts of beef from each other. The bigger cut is the loin: great flavor and desirable tenderness. The smaller is a slice of fillet steak: good flavor and the tenderest hunk of meat in all of bovinity. Grilling a T-bone on a salt block elevates both of these cuts, developing a delicious crust and converting every drop of moisture they release into a salty-umami deliciousness that amplifies the flavor of the loin and accentuates the tenderness of the fillet. When you're portioning servings, make sure to give everyone a piece of each.

1 (10 to 12-inch) square salt block, at least 1½ inches thick

1 large T-bone steak, about 1½ pounds, 1½ inches thick

½ cup peaty Scotch, like Laphroaig 10

2 teaspoons freshly cracked black pepper

1 large green poblano chile pepper

½ garlic clove, minced

2 sprigs thyme

3 ounces Stilton cheese, chopped up

2 tablespoons unsalted butter, softened

2 tablespoons extra-virgin olive oil

Put the steak and Scotch in a large zipper-lock plastic bag, force out any excess air, seal, and refrigerate for at least 6 hours or up to 24 hours.

An hour before you are ready to start grilling, remove the steak from the bag and pat dry. Season on both sides with the black pepper.

At the same time, put the salt block on one side of an unheated gas grill. Heat the grill to low, cover the grill, and warm the block for 20 minutes. Raise the heat under the block to medium and wait another 20 minutes. Raise it to high and wait another 20 minutes. A laser thermometer aimed at the center of the block should register around 550°F. If using charcoal, bank a chimney's worth of red-hot charcoal briquettes to one side of the firebox. Put the block on the grill grate away from the fire and cover the grill. In 20 minutes, add a dozen more pieces of charcoal to the fire and, using grill gloves, move the block so that it is over the new coals. In 30 minutes, your block will be 550°F and ready for grilling.

When the block is hot, put the poblano on the block and sear on all sides until the skin is blistered all around, about 1 minute per side. Remove to a cutting board and set aside to cool.

CONTINUED

Put the steak on the hot block, cover the grill, and sear on both sides, about 5 minutes per side. Move the steak off the block to the cooler part of the grill, cover the grill, and cook for another 5 to 10 minutes for medium-rare (135°F). Remove the steak to a carving board and rest for 5 minutes before serving.

Meanwhile, rub the skin of the poblano chile with your fingers. Remove the stem and seeds and mince the roasted pepper meat. Blend with the garlic, thyme, Stilton, butter, and oil until everything is well-mixed.

Slice the steak and serve, topped with some of the Stilton butter.

FLANK STEAK CHIMICHURRI
WITH SALT-GRILLED ARGENTINE CHICKPEA FLATBREAD

Chimichurri, a mixture of vinegar and herbs, probably originated in Spain but is now the national grilling condiment in Argentina and Uruguay. There isn't much that chimichurri is *not* good on, but pair it with thinner pieces of meat like flank steak, seared hot and fast to juicy perfection on a salt block, and things get crazy. But there's no reason to stop there. Every time there's a salt block on the grill is a time to look beyond your usual grilling routine. Here we salt-grill the Argentine street food staple known as *fainá*, an evocatively spiced chickpea flatbread that turns this flank steak recipe into a full meal.

1 (10 to 12-inch) square salt block, at least 1½ inches thick

CHIMICHURRI

4 cups loosely packed fresh flat-leaf parsley leaves and small stems

2 cups loosely packed fresh cilantro leaves and small stems

1 tablespoon fresh oregano leaves or 1 teaspoon dried oregano

5 garlic cloves, chopped

¼ cup chopped yellow onion

1 small red chile pepper, stem and seeds removed, chopped

½ teaspoon freshly ground black pepper

⅓ cup sherry vinegar

½ cup extra-virgin olive oil

FLANK STEAK

2 pounds flank steak

FLATBREAD

2½ cups chickpea flour

½ teaspoon fine sea salt

3 tablespoons extra-virgin olive oil

2 tablespoons finely grated Parmesan cheese

1 teaspoon freshly ground black pepper

1 teaspoon ground coriander

To make the chimichurri, pulse the parsley, cilantro, oregano, garlic, and onion in a food processor. Add the chile pepper, pepper, vinegar, ⅓ cup water, and olive oil, and process in pulses to form a chunky sauce. Refrigerate for at least 20 minutes or up to 1 week.

Put the steak in a large zipper-lock plastic bag with half the chimichurri. Seal the bag and refrigerate for 2 hours or overnight.

An hour before you are ready to start grilling, put the salt blocks on one side of an unheated gas grill. Heat the grill to low, cover the grill, and warm the block for 20 minutes. Raise the heat under the block to medium and wait another 20 minutes. Raise it to high and wait another 20 minutes. A laser thermometer aimed at the center of the block should register around 550°F.

If using charcoal, bank a chimney's worth of red-hot charcoal briquettes to one side of the firebox. Put the block on the grill grate away from the fire and cover the grill. In 20 minutes, add a dozen more pieces of charcoal to the fire and, using grill gloves, move the block so that it is over the new coals. In 30 minutes, your block will be 550°F and ready for grilling.

To make the flatbread dough, mix the flour, salt, oil, cheese, pepper, and coriander in a mixing bowl. Stir in 1½ cups water and set aside for 30 minutes to allow the flour time to absorb the water thoroughly.

Remove the flank steak from the bag and wipe off any excess marinade. Discard the remaining marinade. Grill on the hot salt block with the grill covered just long enough to brown both sides, about 5 minutes per side. Remove the steak to the other side of the grill where there is no heat source directly below it.

Spoon small flatbreads (about 3 inches across) onto the hot block. You should be able to get 12 pancakes per batch. Cover the grill and cook the bread for 4 minutes, until browned at the edges and tops are dry. Flip the breads (you may have to loosen the edges by holding the spatula upside down and scraping), and remove the flank steak to a cutting board. Cover the grill and cook the breads on their other side. Remove them to a cutting board. Repeat with the remaining batter if needed.

To serve, slice the flank steak across its grain into thin slices and serve with the flatbread and the remaining chimichurri.

ANTICUCHOS WITH CHILE MORITA SALSA

Anticuchos are a common street food in Peru today and consist of a simple kebab of tangy, spiced beef with chile-garlic dipping sauce. In pre-Columbian times, they were made with llama. Slaves brought to the New World by the Spanish made it with beef heart (a practice still common today), while the enslavers preferred choicer cuts. The beef heart version has a firmer, more satisfying texture and is an authentic experience, but the sirloin brings a juiciness that has merits of its own. Whichever you choose, the salt block is the ideal place to cook it. The block sears and salts the lean, marinated meat so deliciously that the only remaining thing to improve the dish further might be to find some llama.

1 (8-inch) salt block for chilling and grilling or 2 (4 by 8 by 2-inch) salt bricks

1½ pounds boneless sirloin (or beef heart), cut into ½-inch pieces

3 tablespoons sherry vinegar

2 teaspoons hot paprika

1 teaspoon freshly ground black pepper

1 teaspoon ground toasted cumin

1 teaspoon ground turmeric

2 morita chile peppers

1 pound tomatillos, husks removed

1 garlic clove, unpeeled

Combine the beef, vinegar, paprika, pepper, cumin, and turmeric in a medium bowl. Cover and refrigerate for at least 3 hours or up to 12 hours.

An hour before you are ready to start grilling, put the salt block on an unheated gas grill. Heat the grill to low, cover the grill, and warm the block for 20 minutes. Raise the heat to medium and wait another 20 minutes. Raise it to high and wait another 20 minutes. A laser thermometer aimed at the center of the block should register around 550°F. If using charcoal, bank a chimney of red-hot charcoal briquettes to one side of the firebox. Put the block on the grill grate away from the fire and cover the grill. In 20 minutes, add a dozen more pieces of charcoal to the fire and, using grill gloves, move the block so that it is over the new coals. In 30 minutes, your block will be 550°F and ready for grilling.

About 40 minutes into heating the block, use it to cook the salsa ingredients. Put the chiles on the hot block and cook until they inflate and start to pop. Transfer to a bowl of hot water and set them aside for 15 minutes to plump and soften.

Meanwhile, finish the salsa by putting the tomatillos and garlic on the block and cooking for a few minutes on each side, until they get black spots and their skins blister. Put them in a blender. Remove the stems from the moritas and add them to the blender. Blend until pulpy and an almost-smooth salsa forms. Set aside until ready to serve.

Skewer the beef on 8 skewers (no need to soak bamboo skewers). Cook on the hot salt block until browned and medium-rare inside, about 3 minutes per side. Serve 2 skewers per person with lots of salsa for dipping.

SHORT RIB
TACOS

Beef short rib is the end cut from a standing prime rib, the most extravagant, boss-is-coming-to-dinner entrée. That's the problem with it; the expense alone means people rarely invite their bosses over. As a boss myself, I figure there's got to be a better way. It just so happens that almost all the prime ribs are now sold as boneless rib eye, and the humble short rib has been left to its own devices. It tastes like prime rib, but it's pretty cheap, just the thing to gussy up a taco. Tossing the meat in spices first and grilling it on a salt block releases a wealth of festive chile aromas that will make work into play and play into a party.

1 (8 to 10-inch) square salt block, at least 1½ inches thick

1 tablespoon smoked sweet paprika

2 teaspoons ground toasted cumin

1 teaspoon ground chipotle chile

2 teaspoons dried oregano leaves

½ teaspoon freshly ground black pepper

2 cloves garlic, minced

1 green poblano chile, stemmed, seeded, and finely chopped

2 pounds boneless beef short rib, cut into small pieces

4 ounces queso Oaxaca or Monterey Jack, shredded

2 cups of your favorite salsa

4 lime wedges, for squeezing

¾ cup sour cream (optional)

8 (8-inch) flour tortillas

1 tablespoon mild vegetable oil, such as canola

Mix the paprika, cumin, chipotle, oregano, black pepper, garlic, poblano, and short rib in a large mixing bowl. Cover and refrigerate for at least 2 hours or up to 24 hours.

An hour before you are ready to start grilling, put the salt block on one side of an unheated gas grill. Heat the grill to low, cover the grill, and warm the block for 20 minutes. Raise the heat under the block to medium and wait another 20 minutes. Raise it to high and wait another 20 minutes. A laser thermometer aimed at the center of the block should register around 550°F. If using charcoal, bank a chimney's worth of red-hot charcoal briquettes to one side of the firebox. Put the block on the grill grate away from the fire and cover the grill. In 20 minutes, add a dozen more pieces of charcoal to the fire and, using grill gloves, move the block so that it is over the new coals. In 30 minutes, your block will be 550°F and ready for grilling.

Put the cheese, salsa, lime, and sour cream each in its own small bowl for garnishing the finished tacos.

CONTINUED

Once the salt block is hot, grill the tortillas on the grill grate around the block until they are spotted with char, about 1 minute per side. Wrap in foil and keep warm.

Toss the short rib mixture with the oil and grill on the hot salt block in 2 or 3 batches just until cooked through, about 3 minutes per batch, turning as needed. Transfer to a serving platter and keep warm.

Serve warm tortillas and garnishes on the side. Allow guests to assemble their tacos as they like them.

BACON BROWNED
PORK BELLY BURGERS

For decades the burger was all about tradition: lettuce, tomato, onion, pickles, ketchup, on a beef patty. Less was more. Then along came the modern burger and lettuce became kimchi slaw, onions became crisped shallots, and the patty became Kobe beef blended with duck foie gras. For all the attention paid to preparations, cooking has remained pretty much the same: griddle or grill. The salt block offers old-schoolers and new-schoolers alike a formidable canvas upon which to paint their burger dreams. Because burgers are quick to release their juices as they cook, we add fat to the salt block before adding the burgers, creating a barrier that modulates the amount of salt picked up by the meat. The result is a miraculously balanced, full flavor that simply cannot be achieved by conventional cooking.

1 (8-inch) salt block for chilling and grilling or 2 (4 by 8 by 2-inch) salt bricks

BURGER MIXTURE

1 pound pork belly, cut into 1-inch chunks

8 ounces lean pork loin or chicken thigh, cut into 1-inch chunks

1 teaspoon coarsely ground black pepper

½ teaspoon fine sea salt

⅓ cup apple cider

FAT
2 slices bacon, halved

TOPPERS

1 sweet onion, cut into ¼-inch-thick slices

1 tart apple, cored and peeled, thinly sliced

4 (¼-ounce) slices sharp cheddar cheese (optional)

CONDIMENTS

3 tablespoons mayonnaise

1 tablespoon white prepared horseradish

1 teaspoon hot pepper sauce

4 burger buns

CONTINUED

You can ask your butcher to grind the meat for you. If you do, skip the first two steps.

Chill the salt block for 1 hour in the freezer. Spread the chunks of pork belly and pork loin or chicken thigh in an even layer on the chilled block; return to the freezer and chill for 15 minutes, until the pork is firm but not solid.

Chop the meat finely in a food processor or by running it twice through a meat grinder.

Transfer to a large bowl. Work the pepper, salt, and cider into the meat with your hands until thoroughly combined. Form into 4 burgers and refrigerate until ready to grill.

An hour before you are ready to start grilling, put the salt block on an unheated gas grill. Heat the grill to low, cover the grill, and warm the block for 20 minutes. Raise the heat to medium and wait another 20 minutes. Raise it to high and wait another 20 minutes. A laser thermometer aimed at the center of the block should register around 550°F. If using charcoal, bank a chimney of red-hot charcoal briquettes to one side of the firebox. Put the block on the grill grate away from the fire and cover the grill. In 20 minutes, add a dozen more pieces of charcoal to the fire and, using grill gloves, move the block so that it is over the new coals. In 30 minutes, your block will be 550°F and ready for grilling.

Put the bacon slices on the hot block and cook until cooked through but not yet crisp, about 3 minutes, turning once halfway through. If bacon fat starts dripping from the sides of the block, mop as needed with a folded paper towel. Be careful not to burn yourself—the fat is hot. Remove the bacon from the block and reserve on a serving platter.

To prepare the toppers, grill the onion and apple slices in the fat on the block until tender, about 3 minutes per side. Remove to the platter with the bacon.

Put the burgers on the block and grill until browned on both sides and an instant-read thermometer inserted into the side of the thickest burger registers 145°F, 4 to 5 minutes per side. If using cheese, put a slice on each burger 1 minute before they're done.

In the meantime, prepare the condiment sauce. Mix the mayonnaise, horseradish, and hot pepper sauce together and set aside.

Serve the burgers on the buns, each topped with a dollop of horseradish sauce, a few slices of grilled onion and apple, and a piece of bacon.

BURGER TABLE

Here is a template for a dozen killer burgers. Follow the same method as the Pork Belly Burgers (page 45), but substitute the ingredients listed in the table. Feel free to use ground meat rather than grinding it yourself. If you do, you can skip the first two steps in the recipe.

BURGER	BURGER MIXTURE	FAT	TOPPERS	CONDIMENTS
All-American Beef	1½ pounds beef chuck 1 teaspoon freshly ground black pepper ⅓ cup milk 1 tablespoon ketchup 1 teaspoon brown mustard	Vegetable oil, to coat burgers and salt block	4 slices American cheese 4 leaves iceberg lettuce, raw 4 slices ripe tomato, raw	⅓ cup Russian dressing
Meatloaf	12 ounces beef chuck 6 ounces pork shoulder 6 ounces turkey breast 1 tablespoon Worcestershire sauce 2 tablespoons ketchup 2 teaspoons brown mustard ¼ cup coarsely grated yellow onion	Vegetable oil, to coat salt block	12 ounces thinly sliced potato, grilled 4 (¼-inch-thick) slices sweet onion, grilled	½ cup tomato sauce
Buffalo Blue Cheese	1½ pounds beef chuck ½ teaspoon crushed red pepper flakes ⅓ cup buttermilk 4 ounces crumbled blue cheese	2 tablespoons melted butter to coat burgers	½ cup raw shredded celery 4 thin slices red onion, raw	½ cup Buffalo sauce
Steakhouse	1½ pounds beef chuck 2 tablespoons Worcestershire sauce 1 teaspoon coarsely ground black pepper 2 tablespoons prepared horseradish 2 scallions, finely chopped	Olive oil, to coat burgers and salt block	4 (¼-inch-thick slices) yellow onion, grilled 4 slices Swiss cheese 4 slices ripe tomato, raw	1 tablespoon steak sauce mixed with 3 tablespoons mayonnaise and 1 teaspoon ketchup
Balsamic Mustard	1½ pounds beef chuck 2 tablespoons aged balsamic vinegar 1 tablespoon brown mustard 1 tablespoon brown mustard seed	Olive oil, to coat burgers	4 slices aged provolone ½ cup giardiniera, chopped	1 tablespoon brown mustard, 2 tablespoons prepared horseradish, and 1 teaspoon balsamic vinegar, mixed with 2 tablespoons extra-virgin olive oil

BURGER	BURGER MIXTURE	FAT	TOPPERS	CONDIMENTS
Sichuan Scallion	12 ounces beef chuck 12 ounces pork shoulder ¼ cup soy sauce 1 tablespoon hot pepper sauce 1 teaspoon minced garlic 1 teaspoon minced ginger 2 scallions, finely chopped	Dark sesame oil, to coat burgers	¼ cup pickled ginger 4 scallions, trimmed and grilled	¼ cup wasabi mayonnaise
Classic Turkey	1½ pounds turkey thigh meat 2 tablespoons ketchup 2 teaspoons brown mustard 1 tablespoon apple butter ¼ cup coarsely grated yellow onion	2 strips bacon, cooked on salt blocks	4 (¼-inch-thick) slices yellow onion, grilled 8 ounces sliced mushrooms, grilled	1 tablespoon chopped fresh flat-leaf parsley, 2 teaspoons other chopped fresh herbs mixed with ¼ cup ketchup
Turkey Guacamole	1¼ pounds turkey thigh meat ¼ pound chorizo ⅓ cup apple cider ¼ cup coarsely grated yellow onion	Mild vegetable oil, to coat burgers	4 ounces Monterey Jack, shredded ¼ cup pickled jalapeño slices 4 (¼-inch-thick) slices red onion, grilled	¼ cup salsa ¼ cup guacamole 2 tablespoons chopped fresh cilantro
Breakfast	1 pound turkey thigh meat 8 ounces mild sausage meat ⅓ cup apple cider 1 tablespoon ketchup ¼ cup coarsely grated yellow onion	2 strips bacon, cooked on salt blocks	4 fried eggs 4 slices ripe tomato, raw	Ketchup, to taste
Chicken Parmesan	1½ pounds chicken thigh meat ¼ cup red wine 1 tablespoon extra-virgin olive oil 1 teaspoon minced garlic ¼ cup chopped shallot, sautéed 1 tablespoon minced fresh herbs 2 tablespoons grated Parmesan	Extra-virgin olive oil, to coat burgers and salt block	8 ounces sliced mushrooms, grilled 4 ounces shredded mozzarella	½ cup tomato sauce 2 tablespoons chopped fresh flat-leaf parsley
Miso Tuna	1½ pounds tuna steak 2 tablespoons shoyu soy sauce 1 tablespoon white miso paste 1 to 2 teaspoons wasabi paste 1 teaspoon chili paste	Dark sesame oil, to coat burgers	¼ cup pickled ginger 4 scallions, trimmed and grilled	¼ cup lemon vinaigrette
Smoked Salmon	1¼ pounds salmon fillet 4 ounces smoked salmon 1 teaspoon minced garlic ¼ cup coarsely grated red onion	Extra-virgin olive oil, to coat burgers	4 slices ripe tomato, raw ¼ cup capers, chopped 12 chives, sliced	4 tablespoons herbed cream cheese

SALT-ROASTED PORK LOIN
WITH JUNIPER CRUST

Grilling pork loin is risky business. The loin promises moist tenderness with every bite. The anticipation has everyone dropping their Frisbees and racing in from the far-flung regions of the yard. But one wrong move at the grill, and you are left with a chewy, dry disappointment—eyes drop to napkins on laps, and the animated conversation drifts off to sober talk of politics. A salt block delivers on the promise of a pork loin, drawing out protein-rich moisture to form an exceptionally crisp crust that does double duty, providing a barrier that retains moisture and delivering wicked-concentrated flavor. Aromatic juniper and garlic push the aggressively salted, juicy simplicity of this dish over the edge, and the drizzle of balsamic seals the deal.

1 (8 to 10-inch) square salt block, at least 1½ inches thick

1 tablespoon cracked black peppercorns

1 garlic clove, minced

3 juniper berries, smashed and finely chopped

3 tablespoons plus 2 teaspoons extra-virgin olive oil, divided

1¾ pounds boneless pork loin

2 cups balsamic vinegar

Julienned zest and juice of ½ lime

Mix the cracked pepper, garlic, juniper, and 3 tablespoons of the olive oil together. Rub the pork with the mixture and set aside for about an hour.

Meanwhile, boil the balsamic vinegar in a small saucepan over medium-low heat until lightly thickened, about ⅓ cup. Remove from the heat and stir in the lime zest and juice. Set aside.

Half an hour before you are ready to start grilling, put the salt block on an unheated gas grill. Heat the grill to low, cover the grill, and warm the block for 10 minutes. Raise the heat to medium and wait another 10 minutes. Raise it to high and wait another 10 minutes. A laser thermometer aimed at the block should register 450°F. If using charcoal, bank a chimney of red-hot charcoal briquettes to one side of the firebox. Put the block on the grill grate away from the fire and cover the grill. In 20 minutes, using grill gloves, move the block so that it is over the coals. In 10 minutes, your block will be ready for grilling.

Put the pork on the hot salt block and cook until the meat is browned on both sides and resilient, but not firm. A thermometer inserted in a thicker part of the pork should register 140°F. Transfer the pork to a cutting board and rest the meat for 10 minutes before slicing.

Cut crosswise into ¼-inch-thick slices and shingle on a platter. Drizzle with the balsamic molasses and the remaining 2 teaspoons of olive oil; serve immediately.

LAOTIAN PORK SALAD (LAAB GA)

Laab—also known as larb and lap—is the national dish of Laos. Variations may be served on crispy rice, sticky rice, and noodles, but the extra-spicy salty zing that comes from grilling up curry-drenched pork on a salt block calls for laab in its salad form. The heat from the salt block volatizes the spices in the curry, and the moisture produced by the meat dissolves enough salt to elevate both the pork and the salad. Topping it off, the smoke from the grill lends a familiar yet exotic warmth that brings the best of Laos right to your backyard.

1 (8 to 10-inch) square salt block, at least 1½ inches thick

1 tablespoon red curry paste

2 teaspoons dark sesame oil

1 pound boneless pork loin or pork chops, finely chopped in a food processor or by hand

¼ cup freshly squeezed lime juice

¼ cup fish sauce (nam pla)

1 tablespoon rice vinegar

1 garlic clove, minced

1 small chile pepper, halved

¼ cup shredded carrot

1 cup finely diced cucumber

¾ cup diced ripe tomato

¼ cup chopped fresh cilantro leaves

8 large perfect lettuce leaves or savoy cabbage leaves

An hour before you are ready to start grilling, put the salt block on one side of an unheated gas grill. Heat the grill to low, cover the grill, and warm the block for 20 minutes. Raise the heat under the block to medium and wait another 20 minutes. Raise it to high and wait another 20 minutes. A laser thermometer aimed at the center of the block should register around 550°F. If using charcoal, bank a chimney's worth of red-hot charcoal briquettes to one side of the firebox. Put the block on the grill grate away from the fire and cover the grill. In 20 minutes, add a dozen more pieces of charcoal to the fire and, using grill gloves, move the block so that it is over the new coals. In 30 minutes, your block will be 550°F and ready for grilling.

Mix the curry paste and sesame oil until creamy in a medium mixing bowl. Mix in the chopped pork; set aside.

Mix the lime juice, fish sauce, ¼ cup water, vinegar, garlic, chile, and carrot in a large mixing bowl.

Grill the pork on the hot salt block in 2 batches just until cooked through, about 1 minute per batch, turning as needed. Transfer to the large mixing bowl with the dressing and keep warm. Mix in the cucumber, tomato, and cilantro. Divide evenly among the lettuce leaves and serve.

MAPLE-DRENCHED
SALT-SEARED PIG CANDY

Recipes for pig candy, the colloquial name for sugar-coated bacon, are so ubiquitously present on hip food sites that featuring it here feels redundant, but again the magic of salt block grilling pushes the merely hip into timeless, classic deliciousness. Maybe it's the irresistible tug-of-taste between sweet and salty, or the way sugar and fat and smoke caramelize on hot salt, or the uncanny way salt blocks develop firm, chewy texture. Or maybe it's just that pig candy on a salt block is so good we cease to care what's hip and what's not.

1 (8 to 10-inch) square salt block, at least 1½ inches thick

⅓ cup firmly packed dark brown sugar

¼ teaspoon cayenne pepper

6 slices thick-cut bacon

¼ cup pure maple syrup

Forty minutes before you are ready to start grilling, put the salt block on one side of an unheated gas grill. Heat the grill to low, cover the grill, and warm the block for 20 minutes. Raise the heat under the block to medium and wait another 20 minutes. A laser thermometer aimed at the center of the block should register around 350°F. If using charcoal, bank a chimney's worth of red-hot charcoal briquettes to one side of the firebox. Put the block on the grill grate away from the fire and cover the grill. In 40 minutes, your block will be 350°F and ready for grilling.

Mix the sugar and cayenne on a large sheet of foil. Coat both sides of the bacon slices generously with the mixture, pressing the mixture into the meat to help it adhere.

When the grill block is ready, put the bacon slices in a single layer on the block. Cover the grill and cook until the bacon crisps on the edges, about 10 minutes. Brush the slices with maple syrup, cover, and cook for another 5 minutes. They will be fairly crisp. Flip and brush the other side with syrup; cook for another 3 to 5 minutes, depending on how crisp you like your bacon. Remove with a spatula, cut into bite-size pieces with sharp scissors, and eat.

SALT-PRESSED GRILLED CUBANO

Cubanos are usually encased in foil prior to grilling and pressing—it helps to keep the edges from crumbling and falling away. But when you're grilling between hot salt blocks, wrapping is counterproductive. The bread toasts up beautifully, with the moisture lurking in the butter that's slathered on picking up just enough salt to push flavor into this sandwich from the outside in. The effect is not unlike an explosion, a Cubano supernova.

4 (4 by 8 by 2-inch) salt blocks

4 tablespoons unsalted butter, softened

1 loaf Cuban (or Italian) bread, halved lengthwise

¼ cup yellow mustard

12 ounces thinly sliced boiled ham

12 ounces thinly sliced roasted pork

8 ounces thinly sliced Swiss cheese

1 large dill pickle, thinly sliced lengthwise

½ cup mojo, bottled or homemade (recipe follows)

Half an hour before you are ready to start grilling, put the salt blocks on an unheated gas grill. Heat the grill to low, cover the grill, and warm the blocks for 10 minutes. Raise the heat to medium and wait another 10 minutes. Raise it to high and wait another 10 minutes. A laser thermometer aimed at the center of a block should register around 450°F. If using charcoal, bank a chimney of red-hot charcoal briquettes to one side of the firebox. Put the blocks on the grill grate away from the fire and cover the grill. In 20 minutes, using grill gloves, move the blocks so that they are over the coals. In 10 minutes, your blocks will be 450°F and ready for grilling.

Spread 2 tablespoons of the butter on one half of the loaf and the mustard on the other half.

Make layers of ham, pork, cheese, and pickles on the buttered half; top with the mustard-spread half. Use both hands to press down on the sandwich to flatten it slightly. Smear the remaining 2 tablespoons of butter all over the outside.

Using grill gloves, arrange 2 blocks end to end. Put the sandwich on the blocks and top with the other 2 bricks, pressing them down to balance them on top of the sandwich. Cover the grill and grill for about 10 minutes, until the bread is toasted and the cheese has melted. Remove the sandwich to a cutting board and cut on an angle into 8 thick slices.

Serve with mojo for dipping.

CONTINUED

MAKES 1 CUP
MOJO

8 garlic cloves, chopped
½ teaspoon coarse sea salt
⅓ cup freshly squeezed orange juice
⅓ cup freshly squeezed lime juice
⅓ cup olive oil
½ teaspoon dried oregano
½ teaspoon toasted ground cumin
¼ cup chopped fresh cilantro
Freshly ground black pepper

Mash the garlic and salt together in a small bowl (made of something with a grain— wood, unglazed ceramic, or stone works best), using the back of a fork. Add the juices, oil, oregano, cumin, cilantro, and black pepper to taste. Whisk to combine. Use as a dip or sauce. Keep refrigerated for up to 3 days.

LAMB SATAY WITH MINT CHUTNEY AND SPICY PEANUT CRUMBLE

I like to joke that I'm more interested in sauces than the foods the sauces are meant for. Satay—grilled spiced meat skewers typically served in Indonesia with peanut dipping sauce—is certainly no exception. Salt blocks offer a solution to the embarrassment of being the person at the table who has eaten all the sauce before others have enjoyed their second dipped bite. As spices on the meat toast, the juices from the meat itself marry with all of the smoky aroma and glaze the kebabs with a sauce of their own. The cooling fresh-herb chutney dip and the sweet crumble of tropical spices and peanuts try—but cannot—overshadow the awesomeness of these super-juiced skewers.

1 (8 to 10-inch) square salt block, at least 1½ inches thick

MINT CHUTNEY (MAKES 1 CUP)
1 cup fresh mint leaves

1 cup fresh cilantro leaves

2 tablespoons freshly squeezed lime juice

1 serrano chile pepper, seeded, stemmed, and coarsely chopped

1 garlic clove, coarsely chopped

½ inch fresh ginger, coarsely chopped

Pinch fine sea salt

SPICE MIXTURE
2 tablespoons coriander seeds

2 teaspoons cumin seeds

1 teaspoon anise seeds

¼ teaspoon cayenne pepper

¼ cup coconut palm sugar

LAMB
1 teaspoon tamarind paste

¼ cup hot water

2 tablespoons finely chopped fresh ginger

2 tablespoons finely chopped completely peeled lemongrass

2 to 4 shallots, finely chopped

1 garlic clove, minced

1 serrano chile pepper, stemmed, seeded, and minced

1 teaspoon ground turmeric

2 pounds boneless lamb leg, well-trimmed, cut into thin 2-inch-long strips

1 tablespoon peanut oil

PEANUT CRUMBLE
1 tablespoon peanut oil

1 cup unsalted peanuts, coarsely chopped

½ teaspoon fleur de sel

CONTINUED

To make the mint chutney, put all the ingredients in a mini food processor and process until almost smooth. Stir in enough water to make the mixture flow, but it should still be thick enough to cling as a dip. Cover and refrigerate. It should be used within 24 hours.

To prepare the spice mixture, heat a cast-iron skillet over medium-high heat for 3 minutes. Remove from the heat. Put the coriander, cumin, and anise seeds in the pan and stir until toasted, about 30 seconds. Remove the spices from the pan and cool. Grind coarsely in a spice grinder or mortar and pestle. Mix with the cayenne and palm sugar; set aside.

To prepare the lamb, mix the tamarind and hot water in a medium-large bowl until the tamarind paste dissolves. Add the ginger, lemongrass, shallots, garlic, chile, turmeric, and 2 tablespoons of the toasted spice mixture. You should have about 1 tablespoon left; reserve.

Toss the lamb strips in the bowl with the tamarind mixture and the oil. Cover and refrigerate overnight.

An hour before you are ready to start grilling, put the salt block on one side of an unheated gas grill. Heat the grill to low, cover the grill, and warm the block for 20 minutes. Raise the heat under the block to medium and wait another 20 minutes. Raise it to high and wait another 20 minutes. A laser thermometer aimed at the center of the block should register around 550°F. If using charcoal, bank a chimney's worth of red-hot charcoal briquettes to one side of the firebox. Put the block on the grill grate away from the fire and cover the grill. In 20 minutes, add a dozen more pieces of charcoal to the fire and, using grill gloves, move the block so that it is over the new coals. In 30 minutes, your block will be 550°F and ready for grilling.

While the block is heating, prepare the peanut crumble. Heat the peanut oil in a large skillet over medium-high heat. Add the peanuts, salt, and reserved tablespoon of spice blend. Stir until the peanuts are darkly toasted and coated with spices. Cool.

Remove the lamb from the refrigerator and skewer the strips on 12 bamboo or metal skewers. (No need to soak the bamboo skewers.) Discard any of the remaining tamarind spice mix. Cook on the hot salt block for about 1 minute per side, until browned and medium-rare inside. Serve with the chutney for dipping and spiced peanuts for scattering.

PORCINI-DUSTED VENISON STEAKS
WITH SPICED BOURBON BUTTER

The best venison I ever ate was in Vermont, years ago. It was winter, and we were standing in my friend's back yard in the snow with hands semi-frozen around icy beers and a blazing maple-wood fire roaring at our feet. A few beers later, when the fire had died down to a huge bed of coals, we tossed strips of venison onto a grate suspended just inches from the heat and seared them for what seemed to be no longer than a heartbeat. My buddy was a lifelong hunter, and he knew what he was doing. It all seemed so simple, but despite all my efforts over the years, it wasn't until I began cooking with salt blocks that I rivaled that wintery best bite—and just maybe beat it. A blistering-hot salt block helps to form a crackling crust while keeping the interior moist and rare. Now it's the only way I cook venison—an example of how innovation can be its own tradition.

1 (8 to 10-inch) square salt block, at least 1½ inches thick

4 teaspoons finely chopped fresh rosemary leaves

2 teaspoons dried thyme

Pinch ground clove

½ teaspoon ground cinnamon

1 teaspoon coarsely ground black pepper

½ teaspoon crushed red pepper flakes

2 or 3 dried porcini mushroom slices, coarsely chopped

8 elk or deer tenderloin steaks, about ½ inch thick

1 cup bourbon whiskey

¼ teaspoon smoked salt

1 tablespoon brown sugar

4 tablespoons unsalted butter

Mix the rosemary, thyme, clove, cinnamon, and peppers in a small bowl. Grind the porcini in a spice grinder into a powder and mix with half of the spice mixture. Rub all over the steaks and set aside, uncovered, for at least 1 hour or up to overnight. If resting longer than an hour, refrigerate the steaks.

An hour before you are ready to start grilling, put the salt block on one side of an unheated gas grill. Heat the grill to low, cover the grill, and warm the block for 20 minutes. Raise the heat under the block to medium and wait another 20 minutes. Raise it to high and wait another 20 minutes. A laser thermometer aimed at the center of the block should register around 550°F. If using charcoal, bank a chimney's worth of red-hot charcoal briquettes to one side of the firebox. Put the block on the grill grate away from the fire and cover the grill. In 20 minutes, add a dozen more pieces of charcoal to the fire and, using grill gloves, move the block so that it is over the new coals. In 30 minutes, your block will be 550°F and ready for grilling.

To make the bourbon butter, boil the bourbon, smoked salt, and remaining spice mix in a small skillet until thickened and reduced to ¼ cup. Be careful, as it is apt to scorch near the end of the reduction. Remove from the heat, strain, and whisk in the brown sugar and butter until a smooth sauce forms. You may need to reheat after straining to get the butter to melt completely. Do not overheat or the butter will separate.

When the salt block is ready, grill the steaks on the hot block just until seared, 2 to 3 minutes per side. Serve with the sauce.

CHAPTER 2

POULTRY

Chickens have a long history of not flying. Their terrestrial orientation traces back to a red jungle fowl that was probably domesticated somewhere on the Indian subcontinent around 5,000 years ago. The red jungle fowl would fly, grudgingly, only as far as it needed to roost. Chickens today can't be bothered to do even that—which, on the surface, seems strange given how much fun (and how helpful for escape) flying must be. But the bird's aversion to the air seems to have paid off, as the planet is now home to about 19 billion of these flightless wonders. Prized for their eggs as well as their meat, chickens are officially God's gift to salt block grilling.

Chickens are awesome, but they are not everything. Other birds, from the flighty ortolan to the mighty turkey, are also superb salt block grilling options. I refer to chicken here because of its universality and familiarity. Chicken is the gateway poultry.

Grilling poultry on salt raises the flavor profile dramatically, by crisping the skin and concentrating flavorful juices inside. Birds can be chopped into service-sized pieces and cooked atop a salt block. They can be spatchcocked or, in medieval fashion, cloven in twain, and then cooked beneath a salt block. Whole poultry has the added advantage of coming with a convenient cavity for fruits, herbs, vegetables, spices, even oysters or sausage to steam as the bird cooks, infusing the meat and the stuffing with flavor. It can be cooked atop a block, which is as simple as it is delicious.

Salt-block-inspired riffs on traditional ways to cook poultry are fantastic and, as a rule, tastier than the salt-block-free alternative. But while we're at it, why not hack a chip off the old salt block and find new ways to unite bird on salt? Never in the 5,000-year history of the chicken has the cavity been stuffed with white-hot salt rocks (or broken-up bits of an old salt block), yet the results are nothing short of astonishing. The hot rocks increase the flavor exchange and speed up cooking. Or why not paillard (pound flat) a boneless chicken part and then cook it between hot salt blocks, building and compressing flavor to the breaking point? Here, the salt subjects the chicken to heat and pressure (the same forces that make diamonds from coal) to flash cook the meat into thin fillets that are firm, juicy, and explosively flavorful.

Unlike four-legged livestock, poultry is sold with its skin on. This tradition is a boon to salt block grillers. It helps to keep the meat moist while cooking, both by forming a protective layer that inhibits drying and also by sheathing a layer of fat that melts into the meat as it grills. Grill poultry with the skin on, even if you are planning to serve it without the skin. But whenever possible, serve with the skin on, as the combination of fat, along with the traces of moisture, offer a crispy, salty contrast to the tender juiciness of the meat.

ATLAS CLUCKED—
CHICKEN GRILLED BENEATH THE SALT OF THE EARTH

If you think your favorite grilled chicken recipe does full justice to the bird, think again. In fact, so many approaches to grilling chicken fail to take into consideration the fact that we need three things to happen simultaneously: moist breast meat, thoroughly cooked leg meat, and crispy skin. Grilling chicken under a salt block accomplishes all of these things with gusto: The hot block on the cavity side of the chicken both seasons and breaks down the connective tissue, releasing flavor into the meat that might otherwise be lost; the weight of the block presses the differently shaped parts into uniformity; and the blast of heat from the fire on one side and the white-hot salt block on the other cooks everything perfectly while sealing in moisture. The combination makes for one mighty chicken.

2 (4 by 8 by 2-inch) salt bricks

1 (4-pound) free-range chicken

2 tablespoons olive oil

4 cloves garlic, halved lengthwise

½ teaspoon coarsely ground black pepper

Juice of ½ lemon

Half an hour before you are ready to start grilling, put the salt blocks on an unheated gas grill. Heat the grill to low, cover the grill, and warm the blocks for 10 minutes. Raise the heat to medium and wait another 10 minutes. Raise it to high and wait another 10 minutes. A laser thermometer aimed at the center of one of the blocks should register around 450°F. If using charcoal, bank a chimney of red-hot charcoal briquettes to one side of the firebox. Put the block on the grill grate away from the fire and cover the grill. In 20 minutes, using grill gloves, move the block so that it is over the coals. In 10 minutes, your block will be 450°F and ready for grilling.

Remove and discard the neck and package of innards from the cavity of the chicken. Place the chicken breast side down on a cutting board. With a large knife or poultry shears, cut down the length of the spine on both sides. Remove the spine. Cut the breast side of the chicken in half lengthwise. You will now have 2 chicken halves.

CONTINUED

Wash the halves in cold water and pat dry with paper towels. Coat with the olive oil and rub all over with the cut sides of the garlic cloves; afterward tuck the pieces of garlic under the edges of the skin. Season all over with the pepper.

Put the chicken halves skin side down on the grill grate directly over the fire and, using grill gloves or thick oven mitts, put a hot salt block on top of each half. Close the grill and cook until the chicken skin is crisp and deeply grill-marked, about 10 minutes. Remove the blocks using the grill gloves, flip the chicken halves with tongs, put the bricks back on top of the chicken, close the grill, and cook until an instant-read thermometer inserted into the inside of the thicker thigh registers 170°F, 15 to 20 minutes.

Remove the salt bricks, transfer the chicken to a clean cutting board, and let rest for 5 minutes before cutting into parts. Drizzle with lemon juice and serve.

ROASTED CHICKEN
STUFFED WITH HOT SALT ROCKS AND FRESH HERBS

Off the bat you might be thinking, "I don't have any salt rocks." Fair enough, but you will, as I'll explain in a minute. Like cooking half a chicken under a salt block, putting salt rocks into the cavity of a whole chicken is another way of cooking from two directions, faster and more evenly. But the serious magic comes from the salty juices that migrate through all the flavorful bones and connective tissues and into the meat, creating mind-blowing flavor without over-salting. So what to do if you don't own any? Either find some online (themeadow.com) or continue to cook other recipes in this book until your salt block develops cracks and eventually breaks apart. Then just hit the pieces with a hammer and keep for all your salt rock needs.

1 (8 to 10-inch) square salt block, at least 1½ inches thick

3 or 4 salt rocks, about 1½ inches cubed

3 tablespoons chopped fresh rosemary leaves

1 tablespoon cracked fennel seed

1 tablespoon dried thyme

2 teaspoons dried marjoram

2 teaspoons rubbed sage

1 teaspoon cracked black peppercorns

1 teaspoon cracked green peppercorns

1 garlic clove, minced

3 tablespoons salted butter, softened

1 (4-pound) chicken, washed and dried

1 tablespoon extra-virgin olive oil

1 cup dry white vermouth

An hour before you are ready to start grilling, put the salt block and rocks on an unheated gas grill. Heat the grill to low, cover the grill, and warm the salt for 20 minutes. Raise the heat under the salt to medium and wait another 20 minutes. Raise it to high under the salt and wait another 20 minutes. Using grill gloves, move the block so that it is directly over the lower heat, keeping the rocks over the high heat. If using charcoal, bank a chimney of red-hot charcoal briquettes to one side of the firebox. Put the block and rocks on the grill grate away from the fire and cover the grill. In 20 minutes, add a dozen more pieces of charcoal to the fire and, using grill gloves, move the block and rocks so that they are over the new coals. In 30 minutes, your salt will be hot and ready for grilling. Using gloves, move the block away from the heat, keeping the rocks directly over it.

Mix the rosemary, fennel, thyme, marjoram, sage, and black and green peppercorns in a small bowl. Mix 1 tablespoon of the herb mixture with the garlic and butter, mashing them with a fork on a clean work surface until well-blended.

CONTINUED

Separate the skin from the breast and legs of the chicken and gently but firmly insert your index finger under the skin at the neck end of the chicken. Move it around, separating the skin from the meat underneath. Gradually ease your whole hand under the skin, loosening the skin from the breast, legs, and drumsticks.

Spoon half the herb butter under the skin and push it evenly over the breast and legs of the chicken by rubbing the skin to spread the butter. Rub the outside of the chicken with the oil.

Put the chicken on the hot salt block. Using tongs, transfer the hot salt rocks into the interior cavity of the chicken. Spoon the remaining herb mixture into the cavity over the hot salt rocks, cover the grill, and cook

until an instant-read thermometer inserted into the thickest part of the breast registers about 170°F, about 45 minutes. If your grill has a temperature gauge, it should stay around 350°F.

Remove the chicken to a large serving platter. Let rest for 8 to 10 minutes.

While the chicken is resting, bring the vermouth to a boil in a skillet and reduce to ⅓ cup; it will be bubbling furiously and ever so slightly thickened. Remove from the heat and swirl in the remaining herb butter.

Remove the salt rocks and wash off for another use. Carve the chicken and serve with the sauce.

ROASTING BIRDS
WITH ROCKS
Here is a template for roasting poultry with salt rocks, inside and out. Follow the method in the recipe for Roasted Chicken Stuffed with Hot Salt Rocks and Fresh Herbs (page 69), substituting the ingredients listed in the table.

RECIPE	BIRD	SEASONING	TIMING	SAUCE
Roasted Herbed Holiday Turkey	1 (10 to 15-pound) turkey	Sage, thyme, parsley, rosemary, garlic, pepper	4 to 6 hours; if using charcoal, add more coals as needed	Replace the vermouth with turkey broth
Chai-Infused Squab with Lime Kecap Manis	4 (1-pound) squab	Whole-leaf chai tea	20 minutes	Kecap manis with fresh lime juice and lime zest (do not cook)
Orange-Rosemary Game Hens	2 (2-pound) game hens	Rosemary, thyme, orange zest, garlic	40 minutes	Replace half of the vermouth with orange juice
Bedouin Chicken	1 (4-pound) chicken	Caraway, coriander, cardamom, turmeric, chile	45 minutes	Add 1 tablespoon white balsamic vinegar to the vermouth
Roasted Turkey with Herbed Hard Cider	1 (10 to 15-pound) turkey	Same as recipe on page 69	4 to 6 hours; if using charcoal, add more coals as needed	Use apple cider and bourbon in place of the vermouth
Honey Hot Pepper Roast Chicken	1 (4-pound) chicken	Orange zest, garlic, rosemary, sage, crushed pepper flakes	45 minutes	Add 2 tablespoons honey to the vermouth and 1 teaspoon hot sauce with the butter

SALT-SEARED CHICKEN PAILLARDS
WITH BALSAMIC-SAGE BUTTER

Nuclear bombs are detonated by creating an explosion around a fissionable core. The pressure and heat from the explosions break apart the atoms, releasing tremendous energy. Think of salt blocks as your detonators and a thinly pounded breast of chicken as your fissionable material. Paillards—thinly pounded sheets of boneless meat—are always the quickest way to cook meat, but pressed between two salt blocks—this is a flavor bomb, pure and simple.

2 (8 to 10-inch) square salt blocks, at least 1½ inches thick

8 garlic cloves, minced

½ cup balsamic vinegar

¼ teaspoon freshly ground black pepper

2 tablespoons unsalted butter

2 (6-ounce) boneless and skinless chicken breast halves

6 medium sage leaves, slivered

An hour before you are ready to start grilling, put the salt blocks on an unheated gas grill. Heat the grill to low, cover the grill, and warm the blocks for 20 minutes. Raise the heat to medium and wait another 20 minutes. Raise it to high and wait another 20 minutes. A laser thermometer aimed at the center of the block should register around 550°F. If using charcoal, bank a chimney of red-hot charcoal briquettes to one side of the firebox. Put the block on the grill grate away from the fire and cover the grill. In 20 minutes, add a dozen more pieces of charcoal to the fire and, using grill gloves, move the block so that it is over the new coals. In 30 minutes, your block will be 550°F and ready for grilling.

While the salt blocks are heating, simmer the garlic and balsamic vinegar in a medium skillet over medium-high heat until the garlic is soft and the liquid has reduced to a glaze, about 4 minutes. Season with the pepper and strain into a small bowl. Smash the garlic remaining in the strainer into a coarse paste with the back of a fork; set aside to cool. Work the garlic mixture into the butter; set aside.

Brush the chicken breasts on both sides with half the garlic butter and sandwich between 2 sheets of plastic wrap. Pound with a flat meat pounder or rubber mallet until even, about a ¼-inch thickness. Do not pound so hard that the meat tears.

Remove one of the sheets of plastic from one of the pounded breast halves. Invert onto your palm and then invert onto one of the hot salt blocks, keeping your hand away from the salt but allowing the chicken to fall flat onto the hot surface. Scatter half the sage leaves over top. Using heavy grill gloves, lift the other block and put on top of the chicken to weigh it down.

Cook for 1 minute. Lift the top block. The chicken should be flattened and cooked through. Remove with a spatula to a serving plate and repeat with the remaining chicken breast. Set a small spoonful of the remaining garlic butter on each slice of chicken. Garnish with more fresh sage if desired.

KOREAN BBQ CHICKEN ON HOT SALT WITH SALT BLOCK BANCHAN

Hot salt blocks are the perfect vehicle for making tabletop restaurant-style Korean barbecue right at home. Heat up the block as you would any grilling recipe. In the meantime, place a hot pad or silicone pot holder on the table and a ceramic trivet on top of that to create a thoroughly insulated spot for the salt block. When the block is hot and you are ready to eat, transfer the block to the table with a metal holder or heavy oven mitts. The block will stay hot enough for two or three rounds of searing. Or just sit next to the grill and enjoy the best Korean barbecue you've ever had right in the great outdoors.

1 (10-inch) square salt block, at least 1½ inches thick

1½ pounds boneless and skinless chicken breasts and/or thighs

3 tablespoons dark brown sugar

2 tablespoons soy sauce

2 tablespoons gochujang

2 teaspoons minced fresh ginger

2 teaspoons dark sesame oil

½ teaspoon crushed red pepper flakes

3 garlic cloves, minced

¾ cup cooked rice

12 butter lettuce leaves

1 cup banchan, store-bought or homemade on a salt block (recipe follows)

3 scallions (green and white parts), trimmed and sliced

Put the chicken on a sheet pan and freeze until firm, about 30 minutes. Slice into ¹⁄₁₆-inch-thick slices. Toss with the brown sugar. Combine the soy sauce, gochujang, ginger, sesame oil, red pepper flakes, and garlic in a large zipper-lock plastic bag. Add the chicken and massage the outside of the bag to get the chicken uniformly coated. Refrigerate for 1 hour.

An hour before you are ready to start grilling, put the salt block on an unheated gas grill. Heat the grill to low, cover the grill, and warm the block for 20 minutes. Raise the heat to medium and wait another 20 minutes. Raise it to high and wait another 20 minutes. A laser thermometer aimed at the center of the block should register around 550°F. If using charcoal, bank a chimney of red-hot charcoal briquettes to one side of the firebox. Put the block on the grill grate away from the fire and cover the grill. In 20 minutes, add a dozen more pieces of charcoal to the fire and, using grill gloves, move the block so that it is over the new coals. In 30 minutes, your block will be 550°F and ready for grilling.

You can cook the barbecue right on the grill or, if you have a large ceramic trivet, you can bring the hot salt block onto the table and grill right on the hot block, as one would in a Korean barbecue restaurant.

CONTINUED

Lift the chicken from the marinade and discard the marinade. Grill the chicken on the hot salt for 1 to 2 minutes per side, until cooked through.

Put 1 tablespoon of rice in each lettuce leaf. Divide the chicken among the leaves. Top each with some banchan and sliced scallions. Serve.

SALT BLOCK BANCHAN

Banchan, the traditional garnishes for Korean barbecue, could be almost anything. Many recipes, however, take time for the salt, acid, and/or fermentation to take action. Quick-curing banchan with salt blocks makes banchan sides a fast addition to any grilled dish.

MAKES 2 CUPS
QUICK KIMCHI

2 (8 to 10-inch) square salt blocks

½ head napa cabbage, coarsely chopped

½ medium red onion, sliced into ¼-inch-thick rounds

1 Kirby cucumber or ½ English cucumber, sliced into ¼-inch-thick rounds

2 tablespoons gochujang

1 tablespoon minced garlic

1 teaspoon dark sesame oil

1 tablespoon toasted sesame seeds

Put one of the salt blocks on a rimmed sheet pan. Spread the cabbage pieces in an even layer on top and set the other salt block on top. Set aside until you can see cabbage water in the sheet pan, about 40 minutes. Lift the top block; the cabbage should be moist and just starting to get tender. Transfer it to a serving bowl.

Wipe off the salt blocks. Do the same process with the red onion and cucumbers; the onion will take about 10 minutes and the cucumbers should be done in 6 minutes.

Add the gochujang, garlic, sesame oil, and sesame seeds; toss to combine. Serve immediately or keep in the refrigerator for up to 1 month.

KOREAN WATERMELON PICKLE

2 (8 to 10-inch) square salt blocks

½ small seedless watermelon, rind and white pith removed

1 medium red onion, sliced into ¼-inch-thick rounds

1 Kirby cucumber or ½ English cucumber, sliced into ¼-inch-thick rounds

2 tablespoons gochujang

1 tablespoon minced fresh ginger

1 garlic clove, minced

1 scallion (green and white parts), cut into 2-inch matchsticks

Cut the watermelon into 3 wedges and cut each wedge into thin slices. Put one of the salt blocks on a rimmed sheet pan. Place as many of the watermelon pieces on top of the block as will fit in an even layer and set the other salt block on top. Set aside until you can see water in the sheet pan, about 10 minutes. Lift the top block; the melon will be tender. Transfer it to a cutting board and repeat with the remaining melon. Cut the pickled melon into small pieces and put in a serving bowl.

Wipe off the salt blocks. Do the same process with the red onion and cucumbers; the onion will take about 10 minutes and the cucumbers should be done in 6 minutes. Chop them into small pieces as well.

Add the gochujang, ginger, garlic, and scallion; toss to combine. Serve immediately or keep in the refrigerator for up to 2 weeks.

GARLIC CHIVE SALAD

10 ounces garlic chives (buchu), root ends trimmed, washed, and dried

2 teaspoons Korean hot pepper flakes (gochugaru)

1 teaspoon doenjang soybean paste

1 teaspoon fish sauce

1 teaspoon dark sesame oil

1 garlic clove, minced

1 teaspoon toasted sesame seeds

Cut the garlic chives into 2-inch-long pieces. Put one of the salt blocks on a rimmed sheet pan. Place as many of the chive pieces on top of the block as will fit in an even layer (no more than ¼ inch thick) and set the other salt block on top. Set aside until you can see water in the sheet pan, about 10 minutes. Lift the top block; the chives will have wilted. Transfer to a serving bowl and repeat with the remaining chives.

Add the gochugaru, doenjang, fish sauce, sesame oil, garlic, and sesame seeds; toss to combine. Serve immediately or keep in the refrigerator for up to 2 weeks.

SALT-GRILLED WARM CHICKEN CORN SALAD

Vivid colors are the name of the game here: golden corn, crimson peppers, magenta raspberries, cherry-red tomatoes, burgundy red onion, and golden browned chicken. What unifies them is the salt block, a cotton candy slab of sizzling hot salt that elevates each ingredient independently and inspires them to join forces to make one delicious salad. The ingredients are grilled in sequence and then combined at the end. It's best served warm, but you can set the finished salad aside in the oven or wrapped in a towel and continue grilling on the block if desired.

1 (8 to 10-inch) square salt block

4 ears corn, in husk

1 red bell pepper

2 (6-ounce) boneless and skinless chicken breast halves

¼ teaspoon freshly ground black pepper

2 tablespoons raspberry vinegar

¼ cup olive oil

1 tablespoon finely chopped tarragon leaves

¼ cup finely chopped red onion

12 cherry tomatoes, quartered

6 ounces fresh raspberries

Half an hour before you are ready to start grilling, put the salt block on an unheated gas grill. Heat the grill to low, cover the grill, and warm the block for 10 minutes. Raise the heat to medium and wait another 10 minutes. Raise it to high and wait another 10 minutes. A laser thermometer aimed at the center of the block should register around 450°F. If using charcoal, bank a chimney of red-hot charcoal briquettes to one side of the firebox. Put the block on the grill grate away from the fire and cover the grill. In 20 minutes, using grill gloves, move the block so that it is over the coals. In 10 minutes, your block will be 450°F and ready for grilling.

Put the ears of corn on the grill away from the fire and the red pepper on the salt block. Cover the grill and cook until the pepper is charred on all sides, about 16 minutes, turning it every 4 minutes. Remove the pepper from the block and let cool. Cover the grill.

While the pepper is cooling, season the chicken breast halves with the black pepper and press down on their thicker ends to make them more or less even with the thinner ends. Put the chicken on the hot salt block and grill until cooked through, with the cover down, about 8 minutes, turning halfway through. Remove the chicken and corn from the grill.

CONTINUED

Rub the skin from the bell pepper, remove the stem and seeds, and cut into ½-inch pieces. Cut the chicken into ½-inch pieces. Peel the husks off the corn and cut the corn kernels from their cobs.

Whisk the vinegar and oil in a serving bowl. Add the tarragon, onion, tomatoes, corn, bell pepper, and chicken. Toss to coat. Carefully toss in the raspberries and serve.

COCONUT BRISTLED
TURKEY BOKA DUSHI

When was the last time you spoke Papiamentu? Odds are, unless you hail from Curaçao, Bonaire, or Aruba, you never have. Papiamentu is an impossible tangle of Portuguese, Dutch, Spanish, French, and English, embellished with flowers of Arawakan and African languages. It sounds like something you would speak instinctively if you were born happy and addicted to cliff diving, or if you learned language from a dancing troupe visiting from some distant purple liquid agave planet. Boka dushi is the Caribbean version of Indonesian satay. *Boka* means "mouth" and *dushi* means "sweet" in Papiamentu. Grilled, these dreamy tidbits on a salt block will teleport your mouth and have you speaking, or at least tasting, a beautiful new language.

1 (8 to 10-inch) square salt block

2 tablespoons molasses

Juice of 2 limes, divided

1 teaspoon toasted ground cumin

1 tablespoon grated fresh ginger

2 teaspoons chili paste, divided

1 garlic clove, minced

1 teaspoon ground turmeric

1½ pounds boneless and skinless turkey breast, cut into 2 by ½-inch strips

⅓ cup coconut milk

3 tablespoons peanut butter

1 plum tomato, finely chopped

1 scallion (green and white parts), finely chopped

2 tablespoons chopped fresh cilantro

1 tablespoon fish sauce

1 teaspoon honey

1 cup unsweetened shredded coconut

Spray oil

Put the molasses, the juice of 1 lime, the cumin and ginger, 1 teaspoon of the chili paste, minced garlic, and the turmeric in a large zipper-lock plastic bag. Add the turkey, turn to coat, squeeze out any excess air, and seal. Refrigerate at least 4 hours or up to 8 hours.

Half an hour before you are ready to start grilling, put the salt block on an unheated gas grill. Heat the grill to low, cover the grill, and warm the block for 10 minutes. Raise the heat to medium and wait another 10 minutes. Raise it to high and wait another 10 minutes. A laser thermometer aimed at the center of one of the blocks should register around 450°F. If using charcoal, bank a chimney of red-hot charcoal briquettes to one side of the firebox. Put the block on the grill grate away from the fire and cover the grill. In 20 minutes, using grill gloves, move the block so that it is over the coals. In 10 minutes, your block will be 450°F and ready for grilling.

To make the dipping sauce, combine the coconut milk and peanut butter in a small saucepan. Stir over low heat until the peanut butter dissolves. Stir in the remaining lime juice and 1 teaspoon chili paste, and the tomato, scallion, cilantro, fish sauce, and honey. Set aside.

CONTINUED

Remove the turkey from the marinade and discard any extra marinade. Spread the shredded coconut out on a plate. Thread 2 pieces of turkey on each skewer and roll in the coconut, thoroughly coating the turkey. Spray each one liberally with oil.

When the salt block is hot, grill as many of the skewers as will fit on the block with space in between until the meat feels firm to the touch, about 8 minutes, turning halfway through. Continue until all of the skewers are cooked.

Serve with the peanut dipping sauce.

SALT-GRILLED
SICHUAN WINGS

The point of salting is to elevate the flavor of foods, except when the point of salting is the salt. Taking chicken wings from their familiar Buffalo home and flying them over prairies and mountains, across six thousand miles of ocean to a jungle coastline, is an opportunity to discard preconceptions about how much flavor a wing can carry. Salt is the fuel that will get you there. The experience is supersonic, so precautions need to be taken, for safety's sake. We bring Sichuan pepper along for the ride, anesthetizing your mouth with its numbing zing, a sort of spicy safety belt that gives you a much-needed sense of security as you zoom.

2 (8 to 10-inch) square salt blocks or 4 (4 by 8 by 2-inch) salt bricks

2 tablespoons freshly ground black pepper

4 teaspoons cayenne pepper

2 tablespoons crushed Sichuan peppercorns

4 teaspoons garlic powder

2 teaspoons ground mustard

3 pounds chicken wings, cut into sections, tips saved for another use

2 tablespoons honey

2 tablespoons hot pepper sauce

2 tablespoons unsalted butter, melted

½ teaspoon fine sea salt

Mix the black pepper, cayenne, Sichuan pepper, garlic powder, and ground mustard in a large mixing bowl. Toss half of the seasoning mix with the chicken wings until well-coated. Refrigerate while the salt blocks heat.

Half an hour before you are ready to start grilling, put the salt blocks on an unheated gas grill. Heat the grill to low, cover the grill, and warm the block for 10 minutes. Raise the heat to medium and wait another 10 minutes. Raise it to high and wait another 10 minutes. A laser thermometer aimed at the center of one of the blocks should register around 450°F. If using charcoal, bank a chimney of red-hot charcoal briquettes to one side of the firebox. Put the block on the grill grate away from the fire and cover the grill. In 20 minutes, using grill gloves, move the block so that it is over the coals. In 10 minutes, your block will be 450°F and ready for grilling.

When the salt is hot, put the wings on the blocks, cover the grill, and cook until they are no longer pink inside, about 10 minutes per side. An instant-read thermometer inserted in the center of one of the bigger wings should register 170°F.

Meanwhile, combine the honey, hot pepper sauce, melted butter, and salt in a large serving bowl. Toss the cooked wings in this mixture and serve.

SALT BLOCK
TANDOORI CHICKEN

India is a big country and may not always have the best relations with its neighbors, but you have to give India credit for the brilliance of its culinary techniques and flavors. Tandoor, India's ceramic wood-fired oven, makes amazing grilled chicken. This is partially because the oven gets so hot but also because the raw ceramic interior draws up surface moisture from the foods inside, making unbelievably crisp crusts. Salt blocks do both of those things, and better. Consider this recipe an open letter to India. Open your borders, make friends, and make the salt blocks from your neighboring Pakistan part of your nation's culinary awesomeness.

2 (8 to 10-inch) square salt blocks or 4 (4 by 8 by 2-inch) salt bricks

1½ cups plain yogurt, divided

2 tablespoons chopped fresh ginger

1 tablespoon sweet paprika

1 tablespoon freshly squeezed lime juice

¼ teaspoon ground habanero or other hot chile

2 teaspoons ground turmeric

3 garlic cloves, minced

4 bone-in chicken leg-thigh quarters

1 English cucumber, peeled, seeded, halved, and thinly sliced

¼ cup chopped fresh cilantro

½ teaspoon toasted ground cumin

¼ teaspoon fine sea salt

Put ¾ cup of the yogurt, the ginger, paprika, lime juice, chile, turmeric, and garlic in a blender and blend until smooth. Pour into a large zipper-lock plastic bag, add the chicken, turn to coat, squeeze out any excess air, and seal. Refrigerate at least 4 hours or preferably overnight.

Half an hour before you are ready to start grilling, remove the chicken from the refrigerator. Put the salt blocks on an unheated gas grill. Heat the grill to low, cover the grill, and warm the block for 10 minutes. Raise the heat under the blocks to medium and wait another 10 minutes. Raise it to high and wait another 10 minutes. A laser thermometer aimed at the center of one of the blocks should register around 450°F. Move the block to the area of lower heat. If using charcoal, bank a chimney of red-hot charcoal briquettes to one side of the firebox. Put the block on the grill grate away from the fire, and cover the grill. In 20 minutes, using grill gloves, move the block so that it is over the coals. In 10 minutes, your block will be 450°F and ready for grilling. Move the block to the area of the grill away from direct heat.

Remove the chicken from its marinade and discard the remaining marinade. Place the chicken on the hot salt blocks, close the grill, and grill for about 45 minutes, turning once, until an instant-read thermometer inserted into one of the thicker thighs registers 165°F.

Meanwhile, mix the remaining ¾ cup yogurt with the cucumber, cilantro, cumin, and salt. Serve the chicken with this raita.

CHAPTER 3
SEAFOOD

Animals that live in water need to be buoyant. To that end, they tend to have delicate skeletons, slightly oily muscles and livers (oil is lighter than water), and innovative systems like air bladders and lateral line systems to position themselves in ever-changing currents. Even though fish move constantly, water supports their weight, so their muscles don't need to be as dense and tough as those of land animals. This is why fish is so tender and flaky. The sophisticated engineering that makes fish so well adapted to their aquatic life is also what makes them delicious.

Fish and salt blocks enjoy an interesting relationship. Salt blocks are the crystallized essence of a great salt sea that evaporated some 600 million years ago, some 50 million years before the Cambrian explosion that gave rise to vertebrates and mollusks. Cooking them on a salt block is about as close as you can get to returning seafood to its maker. But the joys of grilling fish on salt blocks are more than symbolic.

Because sea animals take in saltwater through their gills, they had to evolve a way to maintain the right balance of salt in their bodily fluids. Most saltwater is about 3 percent salt, whereas animal tissue usually can't have a salt content of more than 1 percent. Most fish and shellfish equalize sodium content in their bodies by increasing the amount of amino acids in their muscle tissue. The amino acid glycine is sweet and has an umami (savory) taste. The balance of sweet, savory, and salty created by the blending of amino acids and saltwater is responsible for much of the flavor appeal of seafood. But the 1 percent of a fish that is salt falls far short of what is needed for full flavor.

First, we need a little science. When fish cooks, the muscle fibers contract and the connective tissue softens, resulting in "flaking" (the separation of one layer of muscle fibers from another), which is the sign that fish is cooked. It is important to stop cooking fish as soon as the connective tissue softens. If you keep going, the fish's muscle fibers contract, moisture held in the cells is forced out, and the fish become dry. Collagen, the principal protein in connective tissue, gives seafood a moist, rich mouthfeel—especially shellfish, octopus, and squid. While collagen gives them their richness, it can make them hopelessly tough when overcooked. Our recipe directions always say to stop cooking when a fish appears opaque—a sign that it is cooked, tender, and moist.

Grilling on salt blocks helps to facilitate all of these issues and mitigate the problems with overcooking. Unlike a frying pan, salt reacts in much the same way heat does, breaking down proteins, drawing a small amount of moisture, and then evaporating it off to a salty, crispy potato chip texture that both protects the flesh and contrasts with it. With shrimp, crab, and lobster, the salt dissolves and passes through the shell, where the moisture then poaches the meat evenly as it seasons it. With collagen-rich seafood like scallops, squid, and shrimp, the quick hit of hot salt firms the surface to bring textural contrast, at the same time lending a gentle sear of additional salt. Nature herself couldn't have cooked up fish this delicious—not for another 600 million years anyway.

SALT-BARBECUED SCALLOPS WITH HABANERO SPRINKLE

Scallops—nature's tender umami marshmallows—are perfected with little more than a simple turn on an incendiary block of salt. The heat sears them instantly and the salt sets the surface like a tiny glaze on porcelain. A bare brushing of barbecue sauce increases the stature of the glaze and its slight sweetness is the delicious counterpoint to the seasoning from the salt block. Less is more.

1 (10-inch) square salt block, at least 1½ inches thick

HABANERO SPRINKLE
2 tablespoons sugar

3 tablespoons sesame seeds

Pinch ground habanero chile

¼ teaspoon fleur de sel

BARBECUE SAUCE
2 tablespoons rice vinegar

2 tablespoons kecap manis (sweet soy sauce), teriyaki sauce, or hoisin sauce

2 teaspoons white miso

1 tablespoon orange bitters

2 teaspoons honey

1 tablespoon dark sesame oil

1 garlic clove, minced

½ teaspoon chili paste, preferably sambal oelek

1¼ pounds large wild-caught sea scallops (about 16)

½ teaspoon freshly ground black pepper

2 scallions, roots trimmed and thinly sliced

1 lemon, cut into 4 wedges

An hour before you are ready to start grilling, put the salt block on an unheated gas grill. Heat the grill to low, cover the grill, and warm the block for 20 minutes. Raise the heat to medium and wait another 20 minutes. Raise it to high and wait another 20 minutes. A laser thermometer aimed at the center of the block should register around 550°F. If using charcoal, bank a chimney of red-hot charcoal briquettes to one side of the firebox. Put the block on the grill grate away from the fire and cover the grill. In 20 minutes, add a dozen more pieces of charcoal to the fire and, using grill gloves, move the block so that it is over the new coals. In 30 minutes, your block will be 550°F and ready for grilling.

To make the habanero sprinkle, stir the sugar in a small nonstick skillet set over medium-high heat with a wooden spoon until it liquefies and turns an amber color. Stir in the sesame seeds and cook 30 seconds. Remove from the heat, stir in the habanero and fleur de sel, and scrape onto a sheet pan to cool. When cool and solid, bend the sheet pan and the sesame sheet will pop off. Cut into chunks and pound into rice-grain-size morsels with a mallet.

To make the barbecue sauce, mix the rice vinegar, kecap manis, white miso, orange bitters, honey, sesame oil, garlic, and chili paste in a small bowl. The mixture should be the consistency of heavy cream. If it is too thick, thin with a little water; set aside.

CONTINUED

Pat the scallops dry with paper towels and pull off their white gristly tendons if not already removed. Season the scallops with the pepper and brush with half of the barbecue sauce; let stand at room temperature until the salt block is hot.

When the salt block is very hot (you should only be able to hold your hand above it for a few seconds), place the scallops on the hot block and sear until browned and springy to the touch but still a little soft in the center, about 2 minutes per side. Work in batches if your salt block cannot comfortably fit all the scallops at once.

Remove to a platter or plates and drizzle with the remaining half of the barbecue sauce. Scatter the candied habanero sesame seeds and the sliced scallions over the scallops; serve immediately with lemon wedges.

SALT-SEARED BABY OCTOPUS
WITH SESAME LEAF SALAD AND YUZU DRESSING

A salt farmer in Olhão once invited my family and me to dinner at his favorite restaurant, a refined Michelin-starred affair at the southernmost tip of Portugal. The boys were less than thrilled and looked at themselves in the hotel room mirror—pressed shirt and slacks—with a mixture of bewilderment and disdain. The honey-warm light of the restaurant, soft pillows, and strikingly gentle and unassuming service did nothing to soften their mood. Then came the baby octopus—lightly charred tendrils laced with orange and salt—and the button-down shirts were forgotten. The waiters were taken aback but clearly pleased by the children's tactless requests for seconds, then thirds. Octopus can either be cooked in minutes or hours; either way they are succulently tender, but in between they toughen like galvanized rubber. The Portuguese chef's mastery of this rule left an indelible memory for us. Inspired by that night, we lend this dish an Asian flair and take advantage of the salt block's ability to cook hard and fast. If you can't find baby octopus, small squid can be substituted without any alteration.

1 (10-inch) square salt block, at least 1½ inches thick

2 tablespoons yuzu juice, fresh or jarred

1 tablespoon dark sesame oil

1 tablespoon fish sauce

2 tablespoons rice vinegar

2 teaspoons minced garlic

½ teaspoon coarsely ground black pepper

1 tablespoon olive oil

1 to 2 teaspoons gochujang

16 baby octopus, cleaned, about 1¼ pounds

20 sesame leaves, tough stems removed and cut into thin 2-inch matchsticks

4 scallions (green and white parts), cut into thin 2-inch matchsticks

2 Kirby cucumbers, halved, seeded, and thinly sliced

1 medium carrot, peeled and shredded

CONTINUED

An hour before you are ready to start grilling, put the salt block on an unheated gas grill. Heat the grill to low, cover the grill, and warm the block for 20 minutes. Raise the heat to medium and wait another 20 minutes. Raise it to high and wait another 20 minutes. A laser thermometer aimed at the center of the block should register around 550°F. If using charcoal, bank a chimney of red-hot charcoal briquettes to one side of the firebox. Put the block on the grill grate away from the fire and cover the grill. In 20 minutes, add a dozen more pieces of charcoal to the fire and, using grill gloves, move the block so that it is over the new coals. In 30 minutes, your block will be 550°F and ready for grilling.

To make the yuzu dressing, mix the yuzu juice, sesame oil, fish sauce, rice vinegar, garlic, and pepper in a small bowl.

Mix 3 tablespoons of the yuzu dressing with the olive oil and gochujang in a medium mixing bowl. Add the octopus to the bowl and toss to coat thoroughly. Set aside for 30 minutes.

When the salt block is hot, remove the octopus from the marinade and discard the marinade. Grill the octopus on the hot salt block just until firm, about 2 minutes per side. Transfer with tongs to a serving platter and drizzle with 1 tablespoon of the remaining dressing.

Toss the sesame leaves, scallions, cucumbers, and carrot with the remaining tablespoon of dressing and serve with the octopus.

SHRIMP SOUVLAKI
WITH ANISE TZATZIKI

Greek cooking is ancient and unchanged, hardly evolving at all from its open-fire origins, back when mighty warriors sacked cities for fair maidens and songs were sung and burnt offerings were made to the gods. I like to imagine that *souvlaki*, which is Greek for "little skewers," are snacks eaten by bystanders watching the gladiatorial games held between battles. This dish doesn't just invite such flights of fancy, but it also validates them. Shrimp are seasoned with oil, lemon, garlic, and the national herb of Greece, oregano. Salt enters the dish heroically, with a gallant kiss from the salt-block-seared shrimp, and then again, with radiant force, from lemon wedges grilled alongside the shrimp. Traditionally served with tzatziki, ours is made with fresh anise in place of cucumber. If you can't find fresh anise, go ahead and return to tradition and use thin slices of unwaxed English cucumber.

1 (10-inch) square salt block, at least 1½ inches thick

¼ cup freshly squeezed lemon juice, divided

2 tablespoons extra-virgin olive oil, divided

5 garlic cloves, minced, divided

2 teaspoons cracked fennel seed, divided

1 teaspoon chopped fresh oregano leaves

1 pound jumbo (20 to 25 count) shrimp, peeled and deveined

4 fennel ribs, wide pale-green parts only

¼ cup plain Greek yogurt

1 tablespoon ouzo or other anise-flavored liqueur

¼ teaspoon fine sea salt

½ lemon, cut into 4 wedges

An hour before you are ready to start grilling, put the salt block on an unheated gas grill. Heat the grill to low, cover the grill, and warm the block for 20 minutes. Raise the heat to medium and wait another 20 minutes. Raise it to high and wait another 20 minutes. A laser thermometer aimed at the center of the block should register around 550°F. If using charcoal, bank a chimney of red-hot charcoal briquettes to one side of the firebox. Put the block on the grill grate away from the fire and cover the grill. In 20 minutes, add a dozen more pieces of charcoal to the fire and, using grill gloves, move the block so that it is over the new coals. In 30 minutes, your block will be 550°F and ready for grilling.

Combine 3 tablespoons of the lemon juice, all but 1 teaspoon of the olive oil, 4 of the garlic cloves, 1 teaspoon of the fennel, and the oregano in a zipper-lock plastic bag. Add the shrimp, squeeze out any excess air, and marinate for 30 minutes. No need to refrigerate.

Shave the fennel ribs into tissue-thin slices and mix with the remaining tablespoon of lemon juice, remaining clove of garlic, remaining teaspoon of fennel seed, yogurt, ouzo, and sea salt in a small bowl; set aside.

Remove the shrimp from the marinade and discard the marinade. Cook the shrimp on the hot salt block until firm, about 1 minute per side. Don't crowd the block; grill in batches if needed. Coat the lemon wedges with the remaining teaspoon of oil and grill wherever they fit on the salt block for 1 minute per side.

Serve the grilled shrimp with the tzatziki and grilled lemon wedges for squeezing.

WHOLE FISH SALT-SEARED
WITH PRESERVED-LEMON YOGURT

The sea swims with some 30,000 fish species. You would think exploring this bounty would be irresistible, but just ten fish make up 90 percent of the seafood we eat. Salmon is the number-one choice for grilling. A fillet seared skin side down on a hot salt block on a covered grill is astonishingly good. Most other fish lack the natural oiliness of salmon and don't stand up so well to this treatment. But grill a fish whole, and the flavor and moistness will rival or surpass even the freshest salmon. The salt block crisps the skin like no other method. The gelatin around the bones melts into the flesh, adding flavor and keeping it moist. These facts are an invitation to eat the sea's lesser known but most delicious fish. Fish on the bone on a salt block is the way to go to taste the bounty the sea has to offer.

2 (8 to 10-inch) square salt blocks, at least 1½ inches thick

1 preserved lemon, coarsely chopped, seeds discarded

¼ cup fresh coriander leaves and stems

2 cloves garlic, coarsely chopped

3 tablespoons extra-virgin olive oil, divided

¼ teaspoon freshly ground black pepper

4 whole medium fish with delicious skin (red snapper, pompano, striped bass, etc.), about 1 pound each

¼ cup Greek yogurt

2 tablespoons freshly squeezed lemon juice

Half an hour before you are ready to start grilling, put the salt blocks on an unheated gas grill. Heat the grill to low, cover the grill, and warm the blocks for 10 minutes. Raise the heat to medium and wait another 10 minutes. Raise it to high and wait another 10 minutes. A laser thermometer aimed at the center of one of the blocks should register around 450°F. Turn the heat down to medium to maintain the blocks' temperature, without overheating. If using charcoal, bank a chimney of red-hot charcoal briquettes to one side of the firebox. Put the blocks on the grill grate away from the fire and cover the grill. In 20 minutes, using grill gloves, move the blocks so they are over the coals. In 10 minutes, your blocks will be 450°F and ready for grilling. Move them away from the direct heat.

Meanwhile, process the lemon, coriander, and garlic in a food processor until finely chopped. Scrape into a small mixing bowl and mix in 2 tablespoons of the olive oil and the pepper.

Cut 2 diagonal slices in the sides of all the fish. Fill each slit with 1 teaspoon of the preserved-lemon mixture. Coat each of the fish's cavities with 1 tablespoon of the preserved-lemon mixture. Rub the remaining tablespoon of oil all over the fish.

CONTINUED

When the blocks are hot, put 2 fish on each block, cover the grill, and cook for 4 minutes. Turn them with a large spatula and cook another 3 minutes, until the flesh flakes to gentle pressure. Use the spatula to transfer the fish to dinner plates.

Mix the yogurt and lemon juice into the remaining preserved-lemon mixture. Serve immediately with the lemon-yogurt sauce.

SALT-SEARED
TUNA NIÇOISE

The authentic Niçoise is a beautiful thing, a burlesque of fresh tomatoes, fava beans, black olives, garlic, and herbs intended to disguise the fact that you're eating canned tuna. If you happen to be lounging on a patio with the salt breeze of the silvery Mediterranean tousling the parasols over your head, nothing could be better. But if you're not there, the simple fact is you're eating canned tuna. Flip some fresh fish, thinly sliced potatoes, and green beans on a massive salt block, and let the salt and fire do their work, browning, crisping, and seasoning each to mouthwatering perfection. Toss them on a bed of garlicky, mustardy, acidic greens and Provençal herbs, ignite everything with salty olives and capers, and the word authentic takes on new meaning. This is the authenticity of your own backyard.

1 (10 to 12-inch) square salt block, at least 1½ inches thick

1 large shallot, finely chopped

¼ cup red wine vinegar

2 teaspoons Dijon mustard

1 large garlic clove, minced

½ teaspoon anchovy paste

¾ cup extra-virgin olive oil, divided

1 teaspoon fresh thyme leaves

1 teaspoon chopped fresh tarragon leaves

1 teaspoon dried lavender

1 teaspoon coarsely ground black pepper, divided

2 (6-ounce) tuna steaks, about 1½ inches thick

4 red-skin or golden potatoes, thinly sliced

8 ounces haricot vert green beans or other young tender green beans, stems trimmed

1 head Boston lettuce, broken into leaves

¼ cup drained bottled capers

½ pint grape tomatoes, quartered lengthwise

3 hard-cooked eggs, peeled and quartered

½ cup Niçoise or other oil-cured black olives

8 fresh basil leaves, cut into fine strips

An hour before you are ready to start grilling, put the salt block on an unheated gas grill. Heat the grill to low, cover the grill, and warm the block for 20 minutes. Raise the heat to medium and wait another 20 minutes. Raise it to high and wait another 20 minutes. A laser thermometer aimed at the center of the block should register around 550°F. If using charcoal, bank a chimney of red-hot charcoal briquettes to one side of the firebox. Put the block on the grill grate away from the fire and cover the grill. In 20 minutes, add a dozen more pieces of charcoal to the fire and, using grill gloves, move the block so that it is over the new coals. In 30 minutes, your block will be 550°F and ready for grilling.

While the salt is heating, make the dressing. Combine the shallot and vinegar in a 2-cup measuring cup. Set aside for 15 minutes. Whisk in the mustard, garlic, and anchovy paste. Add ½ cup of the oil, 1 tablespoon at a time, whisking constantly to make a smooth dressing. Stir in the thyme, tarragon, lavender, and ½ teaspoon of the black pepper. Set aside.

Season the tuna steaks with the remaining ½ teaspoon of pepper. Coat the tuna, potato slices, and green beans with the remaining ¼ cup of olive oil.

When the salt is hot, sear the tuna steaks, about 1½ minutes per side. They should still be cold and raw in the center. Remove to a cutting board.

Using grill gloves, move the block to the cooler side of the grill.

Cook the potato slices in a single layer on the block, about 4 minutes per side, flipping with a long-handled spatula. Remove to the cutting board. Depending on the size of your block, this may need to be done in batches.

Cook the green beans in the same way for about 3 minutes per side. Remove to the cutting board.

To assemble the salad, arrange the lettuce leaves on a serving platter. Whisk the dressing and drizzle a bit over the top of the lettuce. Arrange the potato slices and green beans on the bed of lettuce, scatter the capers over them, and drizzle on more dressing. Slice the tuna, arrange, and dress. Place the tomatoes and hard-cooked egg wedges attractively on top, and drizzle all with any remaining dressing. Scatter the olives and basil leaves over all and serve.

GRILLED HALIBUT
GRAVLAX

Gravlax is Scandinavian cured salmon. In a region of fervent lovers of cold fish, gravlax is something like religion, and the scriptures are clear on the subject: Only salmon may be used. Salt blocks extend an invitation not simply to innovate, but to reform. Where gravlax made with granular salt can be mealy and overly salty, the salt blocks' lack of porosity reduces the amount of moisture lost in the process, so the fish cures firmer. Taking this technical improvement as wind in our sails, we substitute halibut for salmon. The mouthfeel is cleaner, way less unctuous, and the firm, pale fish delivers a salinity reminiscent of the open sea. Hit the halibut gravlax with a just a minute over an open fire and the result is worth the heresy.

**2 (8-inch square) salt blocks,
2 inches thick**

1 tablespoon black peppercorns, coarsely ground

¼ cup coriander seeds, cracked

1 orange, zest finely grated, half juiced, half peeled and sectioned

¼ cup sugar

1 halibut fillet, about 1½ pounds, skinned

2 tablespoons extra-virgin olive oil, divided

1 head celery, trimmed, separated into ribs, and thinly sliced diagonally

¼ teaspoon minced garlic

½ teaspoon fleur de sel

½ teaspoon freshly ground white pepper

¼ cup freshly squeezed orange juice

1 orange, 1½ lemons, or 2 limes, or any combination, cut into wedges

Combine the pepper, coriander, orange zest, and sugar in a small bowl. Coat the halibut all over with half the olive oil and then press the spice mixture all over the surface, creating a thick coat. Place the fish on one salt block and place the other salt block on top. You now have a salt-block-and-fish sandwich. Wrap the whole thing in plastic wrap and place on a rimmed sheet pan. Refrigerate until the fish feels resilient but not firm to the touch. This will take 2 hours if you are using a thin fillet and up to 3 hours if using a 2-inch-thick fillet.

When the gravlax is ready, unwrap, remove from between the salt blocks, and pat dry.

Wash off one of the salt blocks and put on an unheated gas grill. Heat the grill to low, cover the grill, and warm the block for 20 minutes. Raise the heat to medium and wait another 20 minutes. Raise it to high and wait another 20 minutes. A laser thermometer aimed at the center of the block should register around 550°F. If using charcoal, bank a chimney of red-hot charcoal briquettes to one side of the firebox. Put the block on the grill grate away from the fire and cover the grill. In 20 minutes, move the block so that it is over the new coals. In 30 minutes, your block will be 550°F and ready for grilling.

While the salt block is heating, prepare an orange-celery salad: Toss the sliced celery, garlic, salt, pepper, orange sections, and orange juice in a medium bowl. Set aside.

Oil the surface of the cured fish with the remaining tablespoon of olive oil. Grill the fish on the hot salt block just until browned on its surface, 1 to 2 minutes per side.

Serve with the salad and slices of the citrus wedges.

MIXED SEAFOOD À LA
PLANCHA DE SAL

Plancha is Spanish for "griddle," and à la plancha is a popular cooking technique for searing food on a flat slab of steel set over an open fire. Steel is fine. It conditions much like cast iron, making for a nice nonstick surface, and the simplicity of cooking à la plancha has an old-world rusticity that makes for great cooking every time. But if iron is rustic and old, a slab of salt is elemental and Paleozoic. And, call me crazy, but I prefer the flavor of salt over the neutrality of steel. Crisped and richly seasoned seafood on a salt block plancha is so simple it borders on flawless, and so flavorful it transcends the ethnicity of any cuisine.

1 (10-inch) square salt block, at least 1½ inches thick

1 lemon, halved lengthwise, divided

½ cup extra-virgin olive oil

8 colossal shrimp, about 8 ounces*

4 small squid, cleaned, about 12 ounces*

8 diver scallops, about 12 ounces*

Freshly ground black pepper

*Substitute any of the seafood options in the table on page 108, using the timing given in the table.

An hour before you are ready to start grilling, put the salt block on an unheated gas grill. Heat the grill to low, cover the grill, and warm the block for 20 minutes. Raise the heat to medium and wait another 20 minutes. Raise it to high and wait another 20 minutes. A laser thermometer aimed at the center of the block should register around 550°F. If using charcoal, bank a chimney of red-hot charcoal briquettes to one side of the firebox. Put the block on the grill grate away from the fire and cover the grill. In 20 minutes, add a dozen more pieces of charcoal to the fire and, using grill gloves, move the block so that it is over the new coals. In 30 minutes, your block will be 550°F and ready for grilling.

While the salt block is heating, squeeze the juice from half the lemon into a mixing bowl. Cut the other lemon half into 4 wedges; set aside. Add the olive oil to the lemon juice in the bowl. Season all of the seafood liberally with pepper and toss with the lemon juice and olive oil mixture.

When the block is hot, grill the seafood in batches on the salt. Avoid crowding the block. Each batch will take about 2 minutes per side. When done, the shrimp will be firm and brightly colored, the octopus will be firm and the tentacles curled, and the scallops will be crispy on the surface and resilient inside. Serve with the reserved lemon wedges.

PLANCHA TABLE

Perfectly pristine seafood can get no better embellishment than a turn over a blazing fire on a searingly hot salt block. The method is straightforward: Procure the freshest sea life you can, toss it with any seasoning you like (other than salt), douse it with good olive oil and a splash of citrus juice, throw it on the hot block just until the meat plumps and its surface crisps, and eat as quickly as possible.

SEAFOOD	TEMPERATURE	TIME
Thick fish fillet (farmed salmon, halibut, cod)	Medium-high	8 minutes
Thin fish fillet (wild salmon, catfish, arctic char)	High	4 minutes
Fish steak	Medium-high	6 minutes
Whole small fish	Medium-high	8 minutes
Shrimp, small to medium	High	3 minutes
Shrimp, large to jumbo	High	5 minutes
Scallops, diver	High	4 minutes
Large squid or octopus, cut into rings	Medium-high	6 minutes
Baby squid or octopus, cleaned, whole	High	4 minutes
Crab, soft-shell	Medium-high	5 minutes
Lobster tail	Medium	8 minutes
Crayfish	Medium-high	6 minutes
Abalone, pounded	High	4 minutes
Mussels, in shell	Medium	6 minutes
Small clams, in shell	Medium	8 minutes
Oysters, in shell	Medium	3 minutes

SUMAC SALMON FALAFEL BURGER
WITH POMEGRANATE BBQ SAUCE

Book yourself a room in the Galata neighborhood of Istanbul. Spend the evening strolling, find a comfortable table on the sidewalk of a crowded side street, and drink a glass of raki, Turkey's famous anise liquor, diluted with ice water and maybe a single ice cube. Rise early, walk into the cool streets, and stop at the first juice cart you encounter, piled high with ice-cold pomegranates. The fresh-pressed glass of juice sends a jolt right down the length of your spine, and any jet lag (or residual raki) vanishes. Walk farther, through the fish market, across the vast plaza of the Yeni Cami mosque, to the legendary spice market, where za'atar is the defining aroma—lemony-bright sumac berries, toasted sesame seeds, and other herbs and spices. These falafel sandwiches capture the essence of exploring a new land, reimagined through the crystalline lens of a glowing hot salt block.

1 (8-inch) salt block or 2 (4 by 8 by 2-inch) salt bricks

BURGERS

1½ pounds salmon, cut into small chunks

1 teaspoon soy sauce

¼ cup hummus

1 garlic clove, minced

¼ cup finely chopped red onion

1 tablespoon ground sumac

POMEGRANATE BBQ SAUCE

½ cup minced yellow onion

1 tablespoon olive oil

1¼ cups pomegranate juice

3 tablespoons molasses

1½ tablespoons raspberry vinegar

3 tablespoons light brown sugar

1 cinnamon stick, broken into 3 pieces

2 tablespoons tomato paste

YOGURT SAUCE

2 tablespoons plain Greek yogurt

1 tablespoon tahini

1 teaspoon za'atar, plus more for serving

2 tablespoons freshly squeezed lemon juice

½ garlic clove, minced

1 tablespoon extra-virgin olive oil

4 pitas, pockets opened

1 cup loosely packed baby spinach leaves

CONTINUED

Half an hour before you are ready to start grilling, put the salt blocks on an unheated gas grill. Heat the grill to low, cover the grill, and warm the blocks for 10 minutes. Raise the heat to medium and wait another 10 minutes. Raise it to high and wait another 10 minutes. A laser thermometer aimed at the center of one of the blocks should register around 450°F. Turn the heat down to medium to maintain the blocks' temperature without overheating them. If using charcoal, bank a chimney of red-hot charcoal briquettes to one side of the firebox. Put the blocks on the grill grate away from the fire and cover the grill. In 20 minutes, using grill gloves, move the blocks so that they are over the coals. In 10 minutes, your blocks will be 450°F and ready for grilling. Move them away from the direct heat.

Chop the salmon finely enough so that when you press some between your fingers it clings to itself, but not so finely that it becomes mushy. You can use a sharp chopping knife and a sturdy cutting board or a food processor. If using a food processor, use the pulse button and be careful to stop processing before the fish purees.

Remove the fish to a bowl and mix in the soy sauce, hummus, garlic, red onion, and sumac until well-blended; do not overmix. Using a light touch, form into 4 patties no more than 1 inch thick. Refrigerate the burgers until the salt block is ready.

Meanwhile, start the barbecue sauce. Cook the yellow onion in the olive oil in a small saucepan over medium heat until soft, about 4 minutes. Add the pomegranate juice, molasses, vinegar, brown sugar, cinnamon stick, and tomato paste, and simmer until lightly thickened and reduced to about ½ cup, about 5 minutes. Let cool.

Make the yogurt sauce by combining the yogurt, tahini, za'atar, lemon juice, and garlic in a small bowl; keep refrigerated.

When the salt is hot, coat the burgers liberally with the olive oil and put on the salt block; cover the grill and cook for 4 minutes. Turn and cook covered until the burgers feel firm, another 3 to 4 minutes.

During the last minute, put the pitas on the grill surrounding the stone and cook until warm and lightly toasted, about 40 seconds per side.

To assemble, spoon a little of the yogurt into each pita, then add the spinach, followed by more yogurt and the burger. Finish with barbecue sauce and a sprinkling of za'atar. If you have any left, you can serve the remaining barbecue and yogurt sauces on the side.

PAELLA ON A SALT BLOCK

Paella is all about the socarrat, the crispy layer of rice and stock that crusts onto the pan and must be scraped up with a large metal spoon or spatula when served. A paella without socarrat is just seafood and rice. Fortunately, a hot salt block makes the development of socarrat crust practically inevitable. The bliss of a properly prepared paella is the confluence of concentrated flavors, toothy textures, and, of course, heady aromas of saffron and herbs. In this version, you get the added advantage of grilling all of the star ingredients on salt blocks before they enter the paella pan. What better setting for tender salt-grilled bites of fresh chicken, chorizo, and shrimp?

1 (8 to 10-inch) square salt block, at least 1½ inches thick, or 4 (4 by 8 by 2-inch) salt bricks arranged in a layer

1 pound boneless and skinless chicken thigh meat

1 pound jumbo (20 to 25 count) shrimp, peeled and deveined

1 pound cleaned squid bodies and tentacles

3 tablespoons extra-virgin olive oil, divided

Freshly ground black pepper

4 ounces uncooked chorizo sausage, cut in half lengthwise

1 cup small diced red onion

1 tablespoon finely chopped garlic

2 cups medium-grain or short-grain rice

1 quart chicken, seafood, or vegetable broth

2 cups canned diced tomatoes, drained

1 bay leaf

1 teaspoon rubbed sage

1 tablespoon tomato paste

1 teaspoon saffron threads

¼ teaspoon crushed red pepper flakes

¾ cup green peas, fresh or thawed

½ cup finely chopped fresh flat-leaf parsley

2 lemons, each cut into 6 wedges

24 medium green olives, preferably Manzanilla

CONTINUED

An hour before you are ready to start grilling, put the salt blocks on an unheated gas grill. Heat the grill to low, cover the grill, and warm the block for 20 minutes. Raise the heat to medium and wait another 20 minutes. Raise it to high and wait another 20 minutes. A laser thermometer aimed at the center of one of the blocks should register around 550°F. Put a large paella pan or heavy iron skillet on the part of the grill that is not directly over the fire. If using charcoal, bank a chimney of red-hot charcoal briquettes to one side of the firebox. Put the block on the grill grate away from the fire and cover the grill. In 20 minutes, add a dozen more pieces of charcoal to the fire and, using grill gloves, move the block so that it is over the new coals. In 30 minutes, your block will be 550°F and ready for grilling. Put a large paella pan or heavy iron skillet on the part of the grill that is not directly over the fire.

In separate containers, toss the chicken, shrimp, and squid in a little bit (1 teaspoon for each item) of the olive oil and season each with pepper. Grill the chorizo pieces in batches on the hot salt block just long enough for them to lose their raw look, about 2 minutes per side. As they are done, transfer them to a cutting board. Cook the chicken next, about 4 minutes per side, with the grill lid down. Transfer to a cutting board. Next, cook the shrimp and squid in the same way, just until they are slightly browned, 2 to 3 minutes per side.

Brush off any food clinging to the block(s) with a wire brush. Put a large skillet or paella pan on the hot blocks. (The blocks diffuse the flames so the paella cooks more evenly.) Add the remaining 2 tablespoons of oil to the pan. Add the onion and garlic, and cook until the onion becomes translucent, stirring often, about 4 minutes. Add the rice and stir for another 30 seconds. Stir in the broth, tomatoes, bay leaf, sage, tomato paste, saffron, some more black pepper, and the red pepper. Close the grill and cook until the rice has absorbed about half the liquid, about 10 minutes.

While the rice is starting to cook, cut the chicken into bite-size chunks, the chorizo into 1-inch lengths, and the squid bodies into rings. Arrange all on top of the cooking rice and scatter the peas over the top. Cover the grill and cook until all of the liquid has been absorbed and the bottom layer of the rice has formed a crust on the surface of the pan, about 15 more minutes.

Remove from the grill and garnish with the parsley, lemon wedges, and olives. Serve immediately.

CHAPTER 4

VEGETABLES AND FRUIT

Salt blocks and vegetables go together like lawns and soccer balls, like shoulders and piggyback rides, like parents away for the weekend and pizza parties. They all exist just fine, the one without the other, but together they spell good times, pure and simple.

Plants are packed with nutritionally vital potassium, but are naturally low in the salt block's equally vital sodium, so together they are nutritionally compatible. The low sodium, high moisture, and occasional bitterness of plants mean they depend on added sodium more than any other food for flavor. On the grill the salt block does double duty. The heat and the salt work together to soften the plant's tough fibers, and the heat caramelizes the edges to create flavorful crispy bits.

Vegetables are pieces of plants that we eat. For cooking purposes they are better identified and categorized by their plant part: leaf, stem, flower, seed, root, or fruit. For instance, beets and carrots are both roots: hard, fibrous, low in moisture, and high in sugar, which is why they are grilled similarly on a salt block. When you heat them, they dry out and take a long time to tenderize. For salt block grilling, root vegetables are best thinly sliced to maximize heat transfer and grilled over moderately low heat, to give the fibers time to slowly soften.

Peppers and peaches are both fruits (soft parts of a plant that house seeds). They are both pulpy, moderately fibrous, and high in both moisture and sugar. Even though we think of them as being radically different, when we think about grilling them, it is helpful to group them together. Fruit, including fruits we consider sweet, like peaches and melons, and those we consider savory, like tomatoes and cucumbers, tend to be juicy. Care should be taken to moderate their release of water on to the salt, and because they can vary widely in fiber strength, the heating of each fruit needs to be considered on its own merits. Grilled tomatoes will collapse in minutes, while crisper apples can withstand a long, slow period on the stone.

Leaves are high in moisture, low in fiber, and filled with air. When you heat them, their fiber collapses, releasing the air and the water, which makes them shrink to nothing—a problem that is exacerbated when grilling on a salt block because the released water dissolves the salt, and then you are basically boiling the leaves in supersaturated saltwater. Leaves are best grilled quickly on superhot blocks in heads rather than as separate leaves, so they brown and have little time to wilt or lose water.

The following recipes can be used as templates for cooking all types of vegetables and fruit. And the first master recipe is designed to be just that. It includes a table with instructions for salt-grilling everything from apples to zucchini.

SALT-BLOCK-GRILLED VEGETABLES
WITH BITTERS VINAIGRETTE

Although salt-block-grilled vegetable recipes vary slightly by heat intensity and timing, the methods are all the same. Trim and cut the vegetables into appropriate sizes and shapes to ensure complete and even cooking, brush them liberally with oil to moderate the amount of salt that gets picked up and to prevent oxidation, and slap them on a hot salt brick. That's all there is to it.

1 (8 to 10-inch) square salt block, at least 1½ inches thick, or several (4 by 8 by 2-inch) salt bricks

VINAIGRETTE

3 tablespoons cider vinegar

1 shallot, minced

2 tablespoons nut oil, walnut or hazelnut

1 tablespoon extra-virgin olive oil

¼ teaspoon freshly ground black pepper

2 tablespoons your choice of bitters: citrus, celery, ginger, cardamom, grapefruit, or any combination

1 teaspoon aromatic bitters

VEGETABLES

1 pound of any vegetable, trimmed and cut for grilling (see table, page 120)

1 tablespoon vegetable oil, such as olive, canola, safflower, grape seed, or corn

Half an hour before you are ready to start grilling, put the salt block on an unheated gas grill. Heat the grill to low, cover the grill, and warm the block for 10 minutes. Raise the heat to medium and wait another 10 minutes. Raise it to high and wait another 10 minutes. A laser thermometer aimed at the center of the block should register around 450°F. Turn the heat down to medium. If using charcoal, bank a chimney of red-hot charcoal briquettes to one side of the firebox. Put the block on the grill grate away from the fire and cover the grill. In 20 minutes, using grill gloves, move the block so that it is over the coals. In 10 minutes, your block will be 450°F and ready for grilling. Using grill gloves, move the block to the cooler side of the grill.

While the block is heating, make the vinaigrette. Put the vinegar and shallot in a small bowl and let sit for 10 minutes while you assemble the remaining ingredients. Add the oils, pepper, and both types of bitters, and whisk to combine.

Arrange the vegetable pieces in a single layer on the hot salt, cover the grill, and cook the amount of time indicated in the table on page 120, flipping with a long-handled spatula halfway through. Depending on the size of your block, this may need to be done in batches.

Transfer to a serving platter or bowl. Whisk the vinaigrette, drizzle over the top, and serve.

VEGETABLE AND
FRUIT TABLE

Here is basic info for salt-block grilling almost any fruit or vegetable. (Note: Some produce, like broccoli rabe or rutabaga, will not cook through on a grill, let alone a salt block.) The preparation column tells basically how you cut it. The heat column indicates the temperature on the surface of the salt block, i.e., 550°F for high, 450°F for medium, 350°F for low. And the time column tells you the total grilling time. Most items are flipped halfway through.

INGREDIENT	PREPARATION	HEAT	TIME
Apple	Peeled, cored, sliced or cut in wedges, oiled	Medium	8 minutes
Apricot	Pitted, halved, oiled	Medium	6 minutes
Artichokes, baby	Halved or sliced, oiled	Medium-low	10 minutes
Asian pear	Peeled, cored, thinly sliced, oiled	Medium	4 minutes
Asparagus	Trimmed, oiled	High	4 minutes
Banana	Peeled, halved lengthwise, oiled, don't flip	High	4 minutes
Beets	Peeled, thinly sliced, oiled	Medium	8 minutes
Belgian endive	Halved lengthwise, oiled	High	3 minutes
Bell pepper	Whole, on 4 sides/Strips, on 2 sides	High	4 minutes per side
Bok choy, baby	Halved lengthwise, oiled	High	4 minutes
Broccolini	Stalks, hard ends trimmed, oiled	Medium	5 minutes
Broccoli	Sliced, hard ends trimmed, oiled	Medium	4 minutes
Brussels sprouts	Trimmed, thinly sliced or shredded, oiled	Medium	4 minutes
Cabbage	Trimmed, thinly sliced or shredded, oiled	Medium	6 minutes
Carrots	Thinly sliced, oiled	Medium	6 minutes
Cauliflower	Broken into florets, sliced, oiled	Medium-low	8 minutes
Celery/Cardoons	Thinly sliced	High	3 minutes
Cherimoya	Cut into wedges, pitted, oiled	High	4 minutes
Chickpeas	Cooked or canned, oiled	High	4 minutes
Chile pepper, fresh	Whole, on 4 sides	High	1 minute per side
Corn on the cob	Husked, whole	Medium	8 minutes
Cucumber	Sliced, oiled	High	1 minute
Dragon fruit	Sliced, oiled	Medium	4 minutes
Edamame	Shelled, oiled	Medium	4 minutes

INGREDIENT	PREPARATION	HEAT	TIME
Eggplant	Whole, on 4 sides/Sliced, on 2 sides	Medium	6 minutes per side
Fava beans	Cooked, oiled	High	5 minutes
Fennel	Thinly sliced, oiled	Medium	4 minutes
Fiddlehead ferns	Hard ends trimmed, oiled	Medium	4 minutes
Fig	Halved, oiled	High	2 minutes
Garlic	Whole cloves	Medium	3 minutes
Green beans, young	Trimmed, whole, oiled	Medium	6 minutes
Hearts of palm	Whole or halved, oiled	High	4 minutes
Leeks	Halved or sliced, oiled	Medium	6 minutes
Lychee	Peeled, whole	High	2 minutes
Mushrooms	Halved or sliced	High	3 minutes
Nectarine	Pitted, sliced, or cut into wedges, oiled	Medium-low	5 minutes
Nopales	Whole, peeled	High	4 minutes
Okra	Whole	Medium	5 minutes
Onions	Sliced, oiled	Medium	5 minutes
Peach	Pitted, sliced or cut into wedges, oiled	Medium	5 minutes
Pear	Peeled, cored, sliced, or cut into wedges, oiled	Medium	6 minutes
Persimmon	Sliced, oiled	Medium	4 minutes
Pineapple	Peeled, cored, sliced, oiled	Medium	5 minutes
Plum	Pitted, sliced, or cut into wedges, oiled	Medium	4 minutes
Potatoes	Sliced, oiled	Medium	8 minutes
Quince (Marmelo)	Peeled, cored, sliced, or cut into wedges, oiled	Medium	5 minutes
Radicchio	Halved lengthwise, oiled	High	3 minutes
Radishes	Halved or sliced	High	1 minute
Romanesco	Broken into florets, sliced, oiled	Medium-low	8 minutes
Star fruit (Carambola)	Sliced, oiled	Medium	3 minutes
Summer squash/Zucchini	Sliced or halved if small, oiled	High	4 minutes
Sunchokes	Sliced, oiled	Medium	6 minutes
Sweet potatoes	Sliced, oiled	Medium	8 minutes
Tomatoes	Thickly sliced, oiled	High	2 minutes
Watermelon	Quartered, rind removed, sliced	Medium	4 minutes

SALT-SEARED
WATERMELON SALAD

Watermelon has a reputation for unadulterated sweetness. In reality it is lower in sugar than any other type of melon. Interestingly, it is also the lowest in sodium, and that lack of sodium to balance its wee dose of sugar is what makes watermelon so unabashedly sweet. A few moments on a wicked hot salt block is all that's needed to bring everything back in balance, taking watermelon from simple and sugary to vibrant and balanced.

1 (8 to 10-inch) square salt block, at least 1½ inches thick

¾ cup balsamic vinegar

2 tablespoons unsalted butter

1 crosswise center-cut slice of a large watermelon, about 1½ inches thick

¼ cup chopped fresh mint, divided

2 tablespoons extra-virgin olive oil

2 tablespoons freshly squeezed lime juice

1 tablespoon pink peppercorns, crushed

1 large ripe tomato, cored and cut into ½-inch pieces

1 English cucumber, peeled, cored, and cut into ½-inch cubes

1 small red onion, cut into ½-inch dice

6 Kalamata olives, pitted and finely chopped

4 ounces ricotta salata, crumbled

In a small saucepan, boil the balsamic vinegar over medium heat until reduced to ¼ cup. Be careful near the end of the reduction; it has a tendency to burn. Remove from the heat and swirl in the butter; cool for 10 minutes.

Remove the green and white rind from the watermelon, then cut crosswise into quarters to make 4 wedge-shaped steaks. Put in a large zipper-lock plastic bag and pour in the reduced vinegar and 1 tablespoon of the mint leaves. Manipulate the bag to get the vinegar mixture evenly dispersed over the watermelon pieces. Press out the air, seal, and let stand at room temperature for 1 to 2 hours.

Half an hour before you are ready to start grilling, put the salt block on an unheated gas grill. Heat the grill to low, cover the grill, and warm the block for 10 minutes. Raise the heat to medium and wait another 10 minutes. Raise it to high and wait another 10 minutes. A laser thermometer aimed at the center of the block should register around 450°F. If using charcoal, bank a chimney of red-hot charcoal briquettes to one side of the firebox. Turn the heat down to medium. Put the block on the grill grate away from the fire and cover the grill. In 20 minutes, using grill gloves, move the block so that it is over the coals. In 10 minutes, your block will be 450°F and ready for grilling. Using grill gloves, move the block to the cooler side of the grill.

CONTINUED

Remove the watermelon from the bag; pour any marinade remaining in the bag into a large salad bowl. Whisk the olive oil, lime juice, and pink peppercorns into the marinade.

Sear the watermelon pieces on the hot salt block for 2 minutes per side. Remove to a cutting board. Slice the wedges in half lengthwise. Cut the slices into ½-inch cubes.

Toss in the salad bowl with the tomato, cucumber, red onion, olives, and remaining 3 tablespoons of mint. Add the cheese and toss lightly. Serve immediately or refrigerate for several hours.

SALT-BLOCK-SMOKED MUSHROOMS
WITH CURRANTS AND PINE NEEDLES

Mushrooms are vegetarian carne, the produce of choice for the knuckle-draggers among vegans who just can't shed the vestigial craving for bold savory flavors. Mushrooms are packed with glutamate, which lends them a beefed-up umami flavor that's hard to find outside of meat. Grilling mushrooms on salt blocks takes them where they want to go. They have a high ratio of fiber to water, so the dehydrating effects of heat and salt collapse their structure and concentrate them quickly, turning sponginess into firmness and mildness into flavor rich enough to satisfy the bone-gnawingist Neanderthal. Huddled around a fire at the mouth of a cave tucked deep in a pine forest, they probably ate this recipe. Any type of unsprayed pine or spruce needles will work. Younger needles (smaller and paler) will be tenderer.

1 (8 to 10-inch) square salt block, at least 1½ inches thick

¼ cup dried currants

1 cup young pine needles or fresh rosemary leaves, divided

12 ounces chanterelle mushrooms (or other wild mushrooms), cut in half lengthwise

2 shallots, thinly sliced

¼ teaspoon freshly ground black pepper

2 tablespoons extra-virgin olive oil, divided

An hour before you are ready to start grilling, put the salt block on an unheated gas grill. Heat the grill to low, cover the grill, and warm the block for 20 minutes. Raise the heat to medium and wait another 20 minutes. Raise it to high and wait another 20 minutes. A laser thermometer aimed at the center of the block should register around 550°F. If using charcoal, bank a chimney of red-hot charcoal briquettes to one side of the firebox. Put the block on the grill grate away from the fire and cover the grill. In 20 minutes, add a dozen more pieces of charcoal to the fire and, using grill gloves, move the block so that it is over the new coals. In 30 minutes, your block will be 550°F and ready for grilling.

While the salt block is heating, put the currants and 2 tablespoons of the pine needles in a small saucepan, cover with water, and bring to a boil. Remove from the heat. Wait 10 minutes and drain.

Put the remaining 14 tablespoons of pine needles onto a sheet of foil.

CONTINUED

Toss the mushrooms and shallots with the pepper in a bowl.

When the block is hot, put the foil sheet of needles right on top of the fire (on the charcoal of a charcoal grill or directly on the heat diffusers of a gas grill).

Coat the surface of the hot block with 1 tablespoon of the oil. Scatter the chanterelles and shallots on the block and sauté until the mushrooms lose their raw look, scraping and tossing with a rigid metal spatula, about 4 minutes. Remove everything and toss with the boiled currants and pine needles and the remaining tablespoon of oil. Serve immediately.

SALT BLOCK LATKES
WITH GRILLED-APPLE SALSA

There are two conflicting ideologies of potato pancakes: soft and creamy or crunchy and shredded. Wars have been fought and food has been thrown. This recipe falls decidedly in the crispy encampment. The hot salt underscores its aesthetics, increasing the crust of the surface while preserving the tenderness of the interior. Latkes are traditionally served with applesauce; the sweet-and-spicy grilled-fruit salsa is a much more dynamic and warlike accompaniment.

1 or 2 (8 to 10-inch) square salt blocks, at least 1½ inches thick, preferably 2

1 pound russet potatoes, scrubbed clean

2 extra-large or large eggs, lightly beaten

2 tablespoons flour or matzo meal

½ teaspoon fleur de sel

½ teaspoon freshly ground black pepper

2 small yellow onions, 1 finely shredded and the other thinly sliced

2 Golden Delicious, Winesap, or Gala apples, peeled, cored, and sliced

2 jalapeño peppers, stemmed, seeded, and halved lengthwise

2 ribs celery, peeled and finely chopped

2 tablespoons chopped fresh cilantro

1 tablespoon vegetable oil

¾ cup sour cream (optional)

Half an hour before you are ready to start grilling, put the salt blocks on an unheated gas grill. Heat the grill to low, cover the grill, and warm the blocks for 10 minutes. Raise the heat to medium and wait another 10 minutes. Raise it to high and wait another 10 minutes. A laser thermometer aimed at the center of the block should register around 450°F. Turn the heat down to medium. If using charcoal, bank a chimney of red-hot charcoal briquettes to one side of the firebox. Put the blocks on the grill grate away from the fire and cover the grill. In 20 minutes, using grill gloves, move the blocks so that they are over the coals. In 10 minutes, your blocks will be 450°F and ready for grilling. Using grill gloves, move the block to the cooler side of the grill.

While the salt blocks are heating, shred the potatoes with the coarse blade of a shredder or food processor. Immediately dump into a large bowl of cold water and swoosh around. The water will turn dirty and pink. Lift the potatoes from the water and put on a clean flat-weave towel. Gather the towel around the potatoes and wring out as much water as you can. Clean the bowl and add the shredded potatoes. Mix in the beaten eggs, flour, fleur de sel, pepper, and shredded onion. Set aside.

Cook the onion and apple slices on the hot block for 2 minutes per side. If there are too many to fit comfortably, work in batches. Remove to a cutting board when done. Cook the jalapeños for 3 minutes per side and move to the cutting board. Close the grill. Chop the apple, onion, and jalapeños finely and toss with the celery and cilantro. Set aside.

Brush the salt block with the oil. Stir up the latke batter. Fry heaping soupspoonfuls of the batter on the hot salt block, flattening the mounds so that they form pancakes of about 3 inches in diameter. Cover the grill. Brown well, about 5 minutes per side. If need be, make another batch to finish up the batter.

Serve the hot latkes with the apple salsa and sour cream, if desired.

SALT BLOCK
BABA GHANOUSH

Some years ago I taught a series of salt block cooking classes on a cruise ship. I lugged 120 pounds of Himalayan salt blocks from my shop in Portland, Oregon, to a small apartment in Dubrovnik, Croatia, before lugging them to port and aboard the *MS Prinsendam*. The 669-foot ship listed decidedly to the starboard as the blocks were wheeled by the porter to my cabin, where they accompanied me to ports in Cyprus, Israel, Turkey, and Greece. When I disembarked in Piraeus for a week of lollygagging in Athens, I hauled two of the remaining salt blocks (the rest I had gifted to a few of the many awesome passengers I had befriended) to a sun-drenched apartment near an open-air market. This is what I made.

1 (8 to 10-inch) square salt block, at least 1½ inches thick or several (4 by 8 by 2-inch) salt bricks

3 garlic cloves, unpeeled

2 slices sweet onion

2 medium eggplants, about 1 pound each

3 tablespoons freshly squeezed lemon juice

2 tablespoons tahini

½ teaspoon freshly ground black pepper

¼ cup extra-virgin olive oil

3 tablespoons chopped fresh flat-leaf parsley

Half an hour before you are ready to start grilling, put the salt blocks on an unheated gas grill. Heat the grill to low, cover the grill, and warm the blocks for 10 minutes. Raise the heat to medium and wait another 10 minutes. Raise it to high and wait another 10 minutes. A laser thermometer aimed at the center of a block should register around 450°F. If using charcoal, bank a chimney of red-hot charcoal briquettes to one side of the firebox. Put the blocks on the grill grate away from the fire and cover the grill. In 20 minutes, using grill gloves, move the blocks so that they are over the coals. In 10 minutes, your blocks will be 450°F and ready for grilling.

Put the garlic cloves and onion slices on the hot block, cover the grill, and cook until soft, about 2 minutes per side. Remove to a cutting board. Put the eggplants on the block, cover the grill, and cook until soft, about 30 minutes, turning every 8 to 10 minutes.

Meanwhile, chop the garlic and onion finely and mix in a medium mixing bowl with the lemon juice, tahini, pepper, oil, and parsley.

When the eggplants are soft, remove from the grill and cool, about 10 minutes. Cut in half lengthwise and scoop the soft flesh from the skin onto a cutting board. Chop finely and mix with the other ingredients. Let rest for 15 minutes to mingle the flavors. Will keep at room temperature for several hours or refrigerated for up to a week.

SALT-SEARED TOFU BÁNH MÌ

French colonists brought some great things to Vietnam when they came to occupy it in 1887: baguettes, pâté, and mayonnaise. They also brought Catholicism, the architectural imperialism of Auguste Henri Vildieu, and the horror known as the French romantic ballad. The one objectively good thing that has come of it is the food. The Vietnamese added fish sauce, cilantro, lime, and barbecued pork to the baguette to make bánh mì. Had the Vietnamese thought to use salt blocks and skip the meat, this is the sandwich we'd all be talking about today.

1 (8 to 10-inch) square salt block, at least 1½ inches thick

TOFU

1 (14-ounce) package extra-firm tofu

1 tablespoon reduced-sodium soy sauce

2 teaspoons dark sesame oil

2 lemongrass stalks, peeled, trimmed, and finely chopped

DRESSINGS

¼ cup hot water

1 tablespoon sugar

¼ teaspoon fine sea salt

¼ cup rice vinegar

1 tablespoon fish sauce

1 medium carrot, peeled and cut into fine matchsticks

2 tablespoons freshly squeezed lime juice

3 tablespoons mayonnaise

2 teaspoons Sriracha

SANDWICH

1 (12-ounce) baguette, halved lengthwise

Spray oil

1 English cucumber, cut in half lengthwise, thinly sliced

6 radishes, thinly sliced

¼ cup fresh cilantro leaves

CONTINUED

Half an hour before you are ready to start grilling, put the salt block on an unheated gas grill. Heat the grill to low, cover the grill, and warm the block for 10 minutes. Raise the heat to medium and wait another 10 minutes. Raise it to high and wait another 10 minutes. A laser thermometer aimed at the center of the block should register around 450°F. If using charcoal, bank a chimney of red-hot charcoal briquettes to one side of the firebox. Put the block on the grill grate away from the fire, and cover the grill. In 20 minutes, using grill gloves, move the block so that it is over the coals. In 10 minutes, your block will be 450°F and ready for grilling.

While the salt block is heating, prepare the tofu by cutting it crosswise into 6 slices. Line a rimmed sheet pan with several layers of paper towels. Put the tofu slices on the towel in a single layer, top with plastic wrap, another sheet pan, and a medium-heavy weight, such as a large iron skillet or 2 large cans of tomatoes. Weight the tofu for 15 minutes.

Meanwhile, mix the soy sauce, sesame oil, and lemongrass in a small bowl. Remove the weight, cover, and towels from the tofu. Brush the tofu with the soy sauce mixture and let rest for another 10 minutes.

To prepare the dressings, mix the hot water, sugar, and salt in a small bowl until the sugar dissolves. Stir in the vinegar, fish sauce, and carrot.

In a separate bowl, mix the lime juice, mayonnaise, and Sriracha.

When the salt block is hot, pat the tofu slices dry with paper towels and cook in a single layer on the hot block, with the grill lid down, for 3 minutes per side. After you flip the tofu, spray the cut sides of the bread with spray oil and put on the grill grate cut side down away from the fire. Remove everything to a platter.

To assemble the bánh mì, put the bottom of the bread on a cutting board and slather with the mayonnaise mixture. Top with a few tofu slices, followed by cucumber, radish, and cilantro. Spoon the vinegar dressing over the top and cover with the bread top. Press down on the bread to make the sandwich more compact. Cut into 6 slices with a serrated knife and serve.

HOT SALTED EDAMAME WITH SESAME, SHISO, AND SICHUAN PEPPER

Beans are fibrous, usually requiring hours of simmering to become edible and soft, but the plump young flesh of green soybeans needs little more than a few minutes on a hot salt block to steam to tenderness. This dish can be prepared on the grill for a more robust contrast of sweet and smoke, or by placing the hot salt block on a ceramic trivet and cooking it tableside indoors alongside the rest of the meal. Or set the table next to the grill and have the best of both worlds.

1 (8 to 10-inch) square salt block, at least 1½ inches thick

1 pound frozen edamame in their pods, thawed

1 teaspoon dark sesame oil

1 tablespoon white sesame seeds

1 teaspoon Sichuan peppercorns

1 teaspoon smoked salt

6 shiso or sesame leaves, stems removed, cut into chiffonade strips

An hour before you are ready to start grilling, put the salt block on an unheated gas grill. Heat the grill to low, cover the grill, and warm the block for 20 minutes. Raise the heat to medium and wait another 20 minutes. Raise it to high and wait another 20 minutes. A laser thermometer aimed at the center of the block should register around 550°F. If using charcoal, bank a chimney of red-hot charcoal briquettes to one side of the firebox. Put the block on the grill grate away from the fire and cover the grill. In 20 minutes, add a dozen more pieces of charcoal to the fire and, using grill gloves, move the block so that it is over the new coals. In 30 minutes, your block will be 550°F and ready for grilling.

While the salt block is heating, blot the edamame with paper towels until they are completely dry. Toss with the sesame oil.

Mix the sesame seeds, Sichuan peppercorns, smoked salt, and shiso in a serving bowl; set aside.

Arrange the edamame pods on the block in an even layer and cook until blistered, about 2 minutes per side, turning with tongs or a sturdy spatula. Transfer to the serving bowl. If needed, cook the edamame in batches. Toss all together and serve immediately. Everyone will peel his or her own.

BLISTERED BABY PEPPERS
WITH DRY HARISSA

Peppers are technically a fruit, and indeed they cook just like pineapple, cherries, and oranges—the hotter and quicker, the better. Get your salt block superhot and let the combination of blistering heat and sizzling salt do its work, producing their unique union of increased tenderness and heightened flavor. Harissa, the ubiquitous hot sauce of Tunisia, is usually blended into a paste. This dried version is perfect for raising the volume of this simple sear of sweet baby bell peppers. Serve them with avocado toasts, tossed with braised collard greens or broccoli rabe, accompanying a salt-seared red snapper, as a condiment with grilled steak, or on top of the Salt-Seared Tofu Bánh Mì on page 131.

1 (8 to 10-inch) square salt block, at least 1½ inches thick

½ teaspoon cumin seeds

½ teaspoon coriander seeds

¼ teaspoon caraway seeds

2 teaspoons crushed red pepper flakes

⅛ teaspoon garlic powder

½ teaspoon smoked paprika

2 garlic cloves, peeled

24 baby bell peppers, yellow, red, and orange

1 tablespoon olive oil

Several pinches large-flake salt

An hour before you are ready to start grilling, put the salt block on an unheated gas grill. Heat the grill to low, cover the grill, and warm the block for 20 minutes. Raise the heat to medium and wait another 20 minutes. Raise it to high and wait another 20 minutes. A laser thermometer aimed at the center of the block should register around 550°F. If using charcoal, bank a chimney of red-hot charcoal briquettes to one side of the firebox. Put the block on the grill grate away from the fire and cover the grill. In 20 minutes, add a dozen more pieces of charcoal to the fire and, using grill gloves, move the block so that it is over the new coals. In 30 minutes, your block will be 550°F and ready for grilling.

While the salt block is heating, put a small iron skillet over medium heat. Add the cumin and coriander and stir until the spices are aromatic and lightly toasted, 2 to 3 minutes. Remove from the heat and cool. Grind in a spice grinder or mortar and pestle with the caraway and red pepper flakes. Transfer to a small bowl and stir in the garlic powder and paprika; set aside.

CONTINUED

When the salt block is hot, cook the garlic clove for 30 seconds per side. Remove from the block and chop coarsely. Put the peppers on the block in a single layer and cook until blistered and spotted with burn on one side, about 3 minutes. Turn and do the same thing on the remaining sides. When done, but while still hot, toss with the oil, ground spices, and a pinch of salt. Take a taste; if the peppers have not picked up enough salinity from the block, sprinkle with some more of the salt to taste.

SALT-STONED BANANAS FOSTER
WITH RYE WHISKEY CARAMEL

Bananas Foster, the elegant tableside confection of stodgy NOLA restaurants, is all about flare and sweetness. This grilled version is flamed just like the original, but its real allure comes from the counterpoint of salt in the searing. The natural sugars in the banana's soft flesh caramelize and crisp and salt at the same time, so at the point you are done cooking, you have a salted-caramel banana. Drizzle them with a boozy caramel of its own, and all traces of stodginess evaporate and your smile is all that's left.

1 (8 to 10-inch) square salt block, at least 1½ inches thick

4 bananas, peeled and halved lengthwise

1 tablespoon freshly squeezed lemon juice

½ cup packed dark brown sugar, divided

¼ cup brewed coffee or chai tea

8 tablespoons (1 stick) unsalted butter

¼ cup rye whiskey

⅛ teaspoon ground Vietnamese cinnamon

1 pint vanilla ice cream

Freshly ground black pepper (cubed pepper is amazing), optional

Half an hour before you are ready to start grilling, put the salt block on an unheated gas grill. Heat the grill to low, cover the grill, and warm the block for 10 minutes. Raise the heat to medium and wait another 10 minutes. Raise it to high and wait another 10 minutes. A laser thermometer aimed at the center of the block should register around 450°F. If using charcoal, bank a chimney of red-hot charcoal briquettes to one side of the firebox. Put the block on the grill grate away from the fire and cover the grill. In 20 minutes, using grill gloves, move the block so that it is over the coals. In 10 minutes, your block will be 450°F and ready for grilling.

While the salt block is heating, brush the banana halves all over with the lemon juice and sprinkle with 2 tablespoons of the brown sugar; set aside.

Bring the coffee to a boil in a large skillet over medium heat. Add the remaining 6 tablespoons brown sugar and stir until it melts. Reduce the heat to low and swirl in the butter, just until melted. When the salt block is ready, take everything except the ice cream and pepper out to the grill.

CONTINUED

Cook the bananas on both sides on the hot block, about 2 minutes per side. Transfer to the skillet. Put the skillet on the salt block and heat until the brown sugar syrup is bubbling. Using a long-handled spoon, lift some of the syrup over the tops of the bananas. Pour the rye into the skillet and stand back; the rye will ignite. Wait for it to burn out; you can douse the flame by throwing a lid on the skillet. Sprinkle the cinnamon over the bananas.

To serve, put 2 banana halves in a large bowl. Top with a scoop or two of ice cream and cover with brown sugar syrup and a sprinkling of black pepper, if using. Serve immediately.

CHAPTER 5
DAIRY

Once in a blissful while, dark rain clouds gather over a thirsty desert plain and let loose. Unfortunately, often enough the rain evaporates before it hits ground, cooked off midair. If only we could crack an egg over an open fire and have it cook and firm up before it hit the grill. Salt blocks fix that naturally. A hot salt block sets up eggs on contact as it draws moisture from the pooling white, forming the thinnest crackled skin at its edge. And it will melt a wedge of cheese and capture every lingering drip.

Unlike other ingredients that benefit from grilling on salt blocks, dairy foods are easily destroyed by high temperature and overcooking. They need steady moderate heat, which means you have to work with your salt blocks a little differently than with other ingredients. In these recipes, you never heat your block at full blast. That means it doesn't take too long to prep your block for grilling, but it also means you have to pay attention. There are two simple techniques that will temper the heat before you add your dairy ingredients:

- Move the block away from direct heat before you start grilling. You can remove the block from the grill and place on a ceramic trivet to cook at the table.

- Lower the temperature of your hot salt block by grilling something else on it first, before you add the dairy ingredient—think hash brown potatoes or bacon before eggs.

As you work through the recipes in this chapter, the tricks for frying eggs and melting cheese over an open fire will become second nature. There are few things better than waking up at your campsite, fanning the embers from last night's fire, and settling in a salt block to preheat while you go for a quick swim in a cold stream. By the time you're dried off, the block is just hot enough to crisp the bacon and fry a brace of eggs. Stoves, nonstick skillets, and anything with an adjustable thermostat are overrated.

SALT BLOCK HUEVOS RANCHEROS

Salt blocks are the Gary Oldman of cooking equipment. Taking on roles that ranged from a drug-addled punk rocker to a circumspect spy to a lustful vampire, he steadfastly puts his characters above his own identity. If Gary Oldman were reincarnated as a piece of cooking equipment, he'd be a salt block: warming the dried chiles to bring them back to life; searing the garlic and onion for the ranchero sauce; acting as a burner for cooking the sauce, a griddle for blistering the tortillas, a skillet for frying the eggs. Bizarrely, Oldman, who has won just about every award known to man, has never won an Oscar. Here's his chance.

2 (8 to 10-inch) square salt blocks, at least 1½ inches thick

2 ancho chile peppers, stems trimmed, seeds discarded

4 garlic cloves, peeled

1 small yellow onion, sliced

1 tablespoon mild vegetable oil, such as canola, divided

1 (14-ounce) can crushed tomatoes

2 chipotle chile peppers, packed in adobo, plus some sauce from the can

¼ cup finely chopped fresh cilantro, plus more for garnish

Up to 8 (6-inch) corn tortillas, 1 or 2 per serving

4 to 8 eggs, depending on whether you want to serve 1 or 2 eggs per person

¾ cup crumbled Cotija cheese

1 lime, quartered

Store-bought refried beans, heated according to package directions, for serving

Half an hour before you are ready to start grilling, put the salt blocks on an unheated gas grill. Heat the grill to low, cover the grill, and warm the blocks for 10 minutes. Raise the heat to medium and wait another 10 minutes. Raise it to high and wait another 10 minutes. A laser thermometer aimed at the center of one of the blocks should register around 450°F. Turn the heat down to medium. If using charcoal, bank a chimney of red-hot charcoal briquettes to one side of the firebox. Put the blocks on the grill grate away from the fire and cover the grill. In 20 minutes, using grill gloves, move the blocks so that they are over the coals. In 10 minutes, your blocks will be 450°F and ready for grilling. Using grill gloves, move the blocks to the cooler side of the grill.

Put the ancho chiles on one of the blocks and heat until flexible, about 10 seconds per side. Remove to a cutting board and cut into strips.

Put the garlic and onion slices on the blocks, close the grill lid, and cook until browned and tender, about 1 minute per side for the garlic and about 3 minutes per side for the onion. Remove to a cutting board and chop both finely.

Put a deep ovenproof skillet on the blocks, and add half of the oil to the skillet plus the tomatoes, chipotles, adobo sauce, ancho chiles, garlic, and onion. Simmer for about 5 minutes. Puree with a hand blender or a standing blender. Stir in the ¼ cup of cilantro; keep warm at the edge of the grill.

Cook the tortillas on the blocks until browned and blistered, but still pliable, about 20 seconds per side. Wrap in foil and keep warm.

Crack the eggs into 4 ramekins or teacups, 1 or 2 eggs per cup.

Brush the tops of the blocks with the remaining ½ tablespoon of oil. Carefully pour 2 to 4 eggs onto each salt block. Pour slowly and try to guide the eggs with a small spatula so that they don't slide off the block. The eggs will start to set up as soon as they hit the salt. Don't worry if a little egg white runs over the edge of the stone. Cover the grill and cook for 3 to 4 minutes, until the white is set but the yolk is still runny.

While the eggs are cooking, set up the plates: Distribute the tortillas among the plates. Top with the eggs. Spoon sauce all around, leaving the yolks exposed. Sprinkle with Cotija and more cilantro. Perch a lime wedge on the side and serve with refried beans.

RACLETTE

Raclette is possibly the single most ingenious milk-based thing ever invented. Its name derives from the French verb *racler,* because the cheese is subjected to heat (traditionally an open fire, but often nowadays a simple electric coil) and scraped off as it melts. Imagine if that Day-Glo orange "nacho sauce" that movie theaters and ballparks pour over chips was actually artisan cheese made from free-roaming Braunvieh cows fattened on sweet alpine clover. Now imagine that instead of stale corn chips, the melted cheese enrobes sweet steaming fingerling potatoes, bread, thinly sliced ham, and pickles. Last, imagine the cheese stoked with just enough salt to leave you too busy eating to imagine anything else. Serve with plenty of chilled Riesling.

1 (8 to 10-inch) square salt block, at least 1½ inches thick

1 (9-inch) round salt block, at least 1½ inches thick

24 new potatoes, red-skin, golden, or fingerling

1 tablespoon mild vegetable oil, such as canola

Freshly ground black pepper

12 shallots, peeled

18 medium-thick asparagus spears

6 slices prosciutto, cut into thirds

12 cornichons (small pickled gherkins)

1 pound raclette cheese, rind removed, cut into 6 slices

Paprika

1 small French baguette, sliced

Brown mustard, for serving

Half an hour before you are ready to start grilling, put the square salt block on an unheated gas grill. Heat the grill to low, cover the grill, and warm the block for 10 minutes. Raise the heat to medium and wait another 10 minutes. Raise it to high and wait another 10 minutes. A laser thermometer aimed at the center of the block should register around 450°F. Turn the heat down to medium. Put the round salt block to one side of the fire. If using charcoal, bank a chimney of red-hot charcoal briquettes to one side of the fire box. Put the square block on the grill grate away from the fire and cover the grill. In 20 minutes, using grill gloves, move the blocks so that they are over the coals. In 10 minutes, your blocks will be 450°F and ready for grilling. Put the round salt block on the cooler side of the grill.

While the salt block is heating, prepare the vegetables: Cut the potatoes into ½-inch-thick slices lengthwise. Toss with half the oil and season with pepper. Cut the shallots into ¼-inch-thick slices lengthwise. Trim the hard ends from the asparagus and wrap each one in a section of prosciutto. Brush with the remaining oil and season with pepper.

Cook everything on the salt block in batches with the cover closed. The potatoes are done when they are fork-tender, about 4 minutes per side; the shallots when they are lightly browned, about 2 minutes per side, and the asparagus when bright green and lightly charred,

CONTINUED

about 3 minutes per side. When the vegetables are done, arrange them around the perimeter of a large heatproof serving platter or board. Scatter the cornichons among them.

Arrange the cheese slices in a circle on the round block and cook until melted and brown on the edges. Using grill gloves, put the round block with its cheese in the center of the platter. Flip the cheese with a sturdy spatula.

To serve, sprinkle the cheese with paprika and place the platter in the center of a table along with the baguette. Give each diner a knife and show him or her how to scrape some melted cheese from the slice closest and spread it on top of his or her choice of vegetables or bread. Eat the pickles and serve the mustard as a condiment.

SALT-GRILLED ROMAINE, EGGS, AND SHAVED PARMESAN

With a valid driver's license, you can rent a 26-foot box truck big enough to hold an Abrams tank. No skills necessary. When you see that guy driving down the road in a 26-foot truck, run for the hills because it's a sure thing he has absolutely zero idea what he's doing. If only grilling lettuce leaves were so easy. On their own, they wilt and burn in seconds, but, kept in a head, the outside may scorch, but the inner leaves remain juicy and take on the flavors of smoke and fire quickly and completely. Grilled romaine is completely different than the raw lettuce you are used to. Instead of watery refreshment, it takes on a meaty corpulence. Grilling romaine on the salt block heightens this effect, crisping and salting and marrying everything together. No skills necessary.

1 (8 to 10-inch) square salt block, at least 1½ inches thick

1 garlic clove, minced

3 anchovy fillets, minced

1 teaspoon brown mustard

5 tablespoons extra-virgin olive oil, divided

Juice of ½ lemon

Freshly ground black pepper

1 head romaine, loose leaves removed, cut lengthwise into quarters

1 ounce Parmigiano-Reggiano, grated

4 large eggs, each cracked into its own ramekin or teacup

½ ounce Parmigiano-Reggiano, shaved

1 teaspoon flake sea salt (optional)

Half an hour before you are ready to start grilling, put the salt block on an unheated gas grill. Heat the grill to low, cover the grill, and warm the block for 10 minutes. Raise the heat to medium and wait another 10 minutes. Raise it to high and wait another 10 minutes. A laser thermometer aimed at the center of the block should register around 450°F. Turn the heat down to medium. If using charcoal, bank a chimney of red-hot charcoal briquettes to one side of the fire-box. Put the block on the grill grate away from the fire and cover the grill. In 20 minutes, using grill gloves, move the block so it's over the coals. In 10 minutes, your block will be 450°F and ready for grilling. Using grill gloves, move the block to the cooler side of the grill.

While the salt block is heating, mash the garlic and anchovies into a paste in a small salad bowl using the back of a fork. Whisk in the mustard and 3 tablespoons of the oil a little at a time to form a thick sauce. Stir in the lemon juice and season to taste with pepper; set aside.

CONTINUED

Coat the romaine quarters with the remaining 2 tablespoons of olive oil and put on the hot salt block. Grill about 20 seconds per side, just until grill marked. Using tongs, transfer the lettuce to the cool side of the grill. Paint with half of the vinaigrette, getting dressing down in between the leaves; sprinkle with the grated Parmesan.

Carefully pour each egg onto the salt block. Pour slowly and try to guide the eggs with a small spatula so that they don't slide off the block. The eggs will start to set up as soon as they hit the salt. Don't worry if a little egg white runs over the edge of the stone. Cover the grill and cook for 3 to 4 minutes, until the white is set but the yolk is still runny.

Put each romaine quarter on a plate. Dress with the remaining vinaigrette and top each with an egg. Scatter the shaved Parmesan over all, plus more freshly ground pepper and a few flakes of salt, if desired. Serve immediately.

GRILLED HASHED POTATOES AND EGGS

You can make perfectly good hash brown potatoes in a skillet, but getting the saline hit from a salt block seared into the surface is worth the culinary juggling act. First ball: You want to grate the potatoes right before you cook them, and squeeze out as much water from the shreds as possible. This helps the potatoes crisp on the outside, but doesn't rid them of so much starchy juice that they don't hold together. Ball two: Microwave them for a few minutes. Pre-cooking the potatoes a little and warming them means that the salt block does what it does best—crisps and salts the surface. If you are philosophically opposed to microwaves (that's me), snap out of it. You can pre-steam the potatoes but you are apt to overcook them, precipitating mushy hash browns. Ball three: Brown the potatoes while the block is hottest, but encourage it to cool down a bit (by moving it out of direct heat) by the time you fry your eggs. Start juggling.

2 (8 to 10-inch) square salt blocks, at least 1½ inches thick

1 pound russet potatoes, scrubbed clean and dried

2 slices bacon

Freshly ground black pepper

4 to 8 eggs, depending on whether you want to serve 1 or 2 eggs per person

Half an hour before you are ready to start grilling, put the salt blocks on an unheated gas grill. Heat the grill to low, cover the grill, and warm the blocks for 10 minutes. Raise the heat to medium and wait another 10 minutes. Raise it to high and wait another 10 minutes. A laser thermometer aimed at the center of one of the blocks should register around 450°F. Turn the heat down to medium. If using charcoal, bank a chimney of red-hot charcoal briquettes to one side of the firebox. Put the blocks on the grill grate away from the fire and cover the grill. In 20 minutes, using grill gloves, move the blocks so that they are over the coals. In 10 minutes, your blocks will be 450°F and ready for grilling. Using grill gloves, move the blocks to the cooler side of the grill.

While the salt blocks are heating, shred the potatoes with the coarse blade of a shredder or food processor. Immediately transfer to a clean flat-weave towel. Gather the towel around the potatoes and wring out as much water as you can. Transfer the potatoes to a plate lined with 2 layers of paper towels. If you want, microwave on high for 2 minutes (not essential but it greatly speeds up the cooking time on the salt block and yields a fluffier interior).

When the salt blocks are hot, put a slice of bacon on each block and cook on one side until the top of the block is coated with bacon fat, about 3 minutes. Remove the bacon and reserve.

Divide the potatoes between the 2 blocks. Using a spatula, press the potato shreds into an even layer. Cook until golden brown on the bottom, about 4 minutes. Flip with the spatula and brown on the other side, about 4 more minutes. Transfer to a heat-safe platter, season liberally with pepper, and keep warm.

Crack the eggs into 4 ramekins or teacups, 1 or 2 eggs per cup.

Return the bacon strips to their blocks, cooked-side up, and cook for another 3 minutes, until the surfaces of both blocks are glazed with bacon fat. Remove the bacon slices. Carefully pour 2 to 4 eggs onto each salt block. Pour slowly and try to guide the eggs with a small spatula so that they don't slide off the block. The eggs will start to set up as soon as they hit the salt. Don't worry if a little egg white runs over the edge of the stone. Cover the grill and cook for 3 to 4 minutes, until the white is set but the yolk is still runny. Transfer the eggs to the platter and top with more pepper. Serve. If you want to give everyone half a slice of bacon, feel free, or eat it all yourself.

SALT STONE ICE CREAM, WALNUT PANCAKES, BITTERED BERRIES

If you are looking for the quickest, simplest, most tried-and-true method for making ice cream, keep looking. But if you are looking for ice cream that calls for techniques that are entertaining and flat-out rad, and brings a riot of flavors together with giddily serious purpose, you are in the right place. Dairy loves salt, and ice cream is no different. Sweet loves salt, too. An ice cream base, spiced and embittered with aromatic bitters, brought to life on a slab of frozen salt, is in a class by itself. Bitterness loves all of the above, and if you don't cook with bitters already, this is your chance. Plunk a scoop on a warm, nutty pancake, drizzle with a sauce of fresh strawberries illuminated by a halo of shining bitter orange, and ask yourself if the adventure was worth it.

1 (10-inch) square salt block, at least 1½ inches thick

12 strawberries, greens removed and berries chopped

¼ cup sugar, plus 1 teaspoon, divided

1 tablespoon orange bitters

⅓ cup finely ground walnuts

⅓ cup whole-wheat flour

⅓ cup unbleached all-purpose flour

1 teaspoon baking powder

½ teaspoon baking soda

¼ teaspoon fleur de sel

1 large egg, separated

1 cup buttermilk

1 teaspoon pure vanilla extract

2 tablespoons unsalted butter, melted

Mild vegetable oil, for coating salt block

1 pint Salt Block Aromatic Bitters Ice Cream (recipe follows)

Half an hour before you are ready to start grilling, put the salt block on an unheated gas grill. Heat the grill to low, cover the grill, and warm the block for 10 minutes. Raise the heat to medium and wait another 10 minutes. Raise it to high and wait another 10 minutes. A laser thermometer aimed at the center of the block should register around 450°F. Turn the heat down to medium. If using charcoal, bank a chimney of red-hot charcoal briquettes to one side of the firebox. Put the block on the grill grate away from the fire and cover the grill. In 20 minutes, using grill gloves, move the block so that it is over the coals. In 10 minutes, your block will be 450°F and ready for grilling. Using grill gloves, move the block to the cooler side of the grill.

While the salt block is heating, assemble the berries: Mix the strawberries and ¼ cup of the sugar in a bowl; set aside for 10 minutes until the strawberries soften and the sugar dissolves. Stir in the bitters; set aside.

To make the pancake batter, combine the ground walnuts, whole-wheat flour, all-purpose flour, baking powder, baking soda, the remaining 1 teaspoon of sugar, and salt in a mixing bowl. Add the egg yolk, buttermilk, and vanilla extract, and stir to moisten everything. Stir in the melted butter.

In a clean separate bowl, beat the egg white using a large whisk until it forms soft peaks (just holds a shape). Do not overbeat. Fold into the batter.

Coat the surface of the hot block with a thin film of oil. Spoon small pancakes onto the hot block, leaving about 1 inch between the pancakes. Cook until brown on the bottom and set up at the sides, about 2 minutes. Flip and cook on the other side until puffed and browned on the bottom. Transfer to a plate with a spatula and keep warm. Cook the remaining batter and serve the pancakes topped with scoops of bitters ice cream and some of the strawberry sauce.

MAKES 1 QUART
SALT BLOCK AROMATIC BITTERS ICE CREAM

1 (8 to 10-inch) square salt block

3 cups half-and-half
2/3 cup sugar
4 extra-large egg yolks
1/4 cup aromatic bitters
1/4 teaspoon pure vanilla extract

Put the salt block in the freezer for at least 4 hours or up to several days.

Heat the half-and-half and sugar in a medium saucepan over medium heat, until tiny bubbles form at the edges of the pan, 3 to 4 minutes.

Remove from the heat. Slowly mix the hot half-and-half into the egg yolks in a small mixing bowl and then stir that mixture back into the saucepan. Cook over medium-low heat, stirring constantly until lightly thickened (180°F). Remove from the heat and cool for 10 minutes. Stir in the bitters and the vanilla.

Cover and refrigerate until thoroughly chilled. Freeze for 30 minutes, until frozen around the edges. Stir to combine frozen and cold custard. Pour a portion of the cold custard onto the frozen block and slough with a sturdy rubber spatula until the ice cream sets up. Transfer to a 1-quart container, seal, and freeze. Repeat with the remaining custard mixture. First slough on the refrozen salt block and store in the same container until ready to serve. Will keep in the freezer for up to 2 weeks.

CHAPTER 6
DOUGH

They say doughs are a mixture of flour and water, but really they are memories. Possibly the most captivating memory of my childhood is awaking at my grandma's old house in Connecticut surrounded by handmade furniture and pictures that were my mother's as a girl. The autumn sun through fall foliage cast a web of gold and crimson on the quilt, and the smell of bacon and sizzling butter and blueberry pancakes on the griddle wafted up from the kitchen. Or I think of another day at dusk in Liguria decades later, diving off rocks into turquoise waters with my sons, sitting sandy-footed next to an outdoor wood-fired oven, and ravenously eating a charred, opulently stuffed calzone with a glass of cold white wine. Both of these are committed to my permanent memories.

The earliest breads were baked directly on a flat stone set over a fire, which means that baking on a salt block on a grill takes us back to the roots of baking. Pita, pizza, focaccia, naan, lavash, and even pretzels are examples of simple leavened flatbreads that bake well on a salt block. The thinner the bread, the hotter the block can be. Lavash, the paper-thin sheet bread of the Caucasus, bakes for about 30 seconds per side. Medium-thick breads, like pizza and naan, bake on medium-hot blocks, and thicker breads, like focaccia and pretzels, are baked either over direct low heat or by placing the block away from the heat of a hot fire.

Adding fat, like oil, butter, or rendered bacon drippings, makes dough tender. Baked goods made with more fat, such as cakes, biscuits, cookies, pastries, and shortbreads, are softer or flakier than low-fat yeast-risen flatbreads. Fat keeps water from hydrating the flour proteins that form gluten, so the gluten strands are shorter (hence the term "shortening") and less elastic. The higher the proportion of fat, the more pronounced that effect will be. Small pastries, like shortbreads and pastry straws, or thin pastries, like tarts and quiches, bake on a salt block beautifully.

Sugar added to dough doesn't just make it sweet. Sugar makes baked goods tender, moist, and crisp and gives them a rich brown color. Remove sugar from a cake or cookie recipe and the results will be dense, dry, and pale. Add extra sugar and the baked good will become crisper and browner. Very sweet cakes and cookies, which come off very crisp, tend to burn on the grill. For that reason, the recipes that work best are chewy cookies, like oatmeal, molasses, or chocolate chippers.

HIMALAYAN-SALT BAKED NAAN WITH SWEET CURRY BUTTER

Naan, the yeasted flatbreads of central Asia, are traditionally baked in wood-fired tandoors, large vertical ceramic ovens that get superhot—hot enough to sear the surface of bread in seconds. This is a rustic cuisine that has been so thoroughly perfected it seems refined. Although home cooks try to duplicate the effects of a tandoor by lining the floor of a conventional oven with ceramic tiles, the heat is never the same. But a salt block heated to incendiary heights over an open fire not only delivers rustic tandoor heat, but also lends just a lick of elegant saltiness. Consider grilling this recipe before or after grilling something else on a salt block, like Lamb Satay with Mint Chutney and Spicy Peanut Crumble (page 59) or Chai-Infused Squab with Lime Kecap Manis (page 71), which are delicious served with the naan.

1 (10-inch) square salt block, at least 1½ inches thick, or other large salt block

1 teaspoon active dry yeast

¾ cup hot tap water (120°F), divided

½ cup plain yogurt

1½ teaspoons ground coriander seeds, divided

1½ cups bread flour

1 tablespoon canola oil, plus more for coating

2 teaspoons sugar

Pinch finely ground kala namak (Indian black salt), plus more for sprinkling

1 cup (approximately) whole-wheat flour

1 tablespoon curry powder

¼ cup milk

2 teaspoons honey

6 tablespoons unsalted butter, softened, divided

Mix the yeast and ¼ cup of the hot water in a large bowl until the yeast is dissolved, about 3 minutes.

Mix the yogurt, 1 teaspoon of the coriander, and the remaining ½ cup hot water in a medium bowl and stir into the yeast mixture until everything is blended. Add the bread flour and stir vigorously for 2 minutes. Cover loosely with plastic wrap and set aside at room temperature until bubbly, about 30 minutes.

Stir in the 1 tablespoon of oil, the sugar, salt, and enough of the whole-wheat flour to make a kneadable dough. Knead on a clean work surface, using additional flour to keep the dough from sticking, until the dough is smooth and elastic.

Wash out the large bowl and coat it lightly with oil. Turn the dough in the oiled bowl to coat with oil; cover with plastic wrap and let rise at room temperature until doubled in bulk, about 1 hour.

An hour before you are ready to start grilling, put the salt block on an unheated gas grill. Heat the grill to low, cover the grill, and warm the block for 20 minutes. Raise the heat to medium and wait another 20 minutes. Raise it to high and wait another 20 minutes. A laser thermometer aimed at the center of the block should register around 550°F. If using charcoal, bank a chimney of red-hot charcoal briquettes to one side of the firebox. Put the block on the grill grate away from the fire and cover the grill. In 20 minutes, add a dozen more pieces of charcoal to the fire and, using grill gloves, move the block so that it is over the new coals. In 30 minutes, your block will be 550°F and ready for grilling.

While the salt block is heating, prepare the curry butter by heating the curry powder, milk, and honey in a small saucepan over medium heat. Remove from the heat and let cool. When room temperature, mix with 4 tablespoons of the butter; set aside.

Divide the dough into 4 pieces; roll each into a ball and flatten into a ½-inch-thick disk. Cover with a kitchen towel and rest for 5 minutes.

Lightly flour a clean work surface and roll each disk of dough into a long oval (about 9 inches long and about ¼ inch thickness). Coat each bread with canola oil and stack on a plate to transport to the grill.

Put one of the breads on the hot salt block and bake until browned and puffed, about 4 minutes. Remove with a tongs and repeat with the remaining 3 breads. As soon as each bread comes off the grill, brush with the remaining 2 tablespoons of softened butter and sprinkle with a little of the remaining ½ teaspoon of ground coriander and a pinch of kala namak.

Serve warm with the curry butter.

SALTY-SMOKY
WALNUT-CHOCOLATE-
CHUNK COOKIES

Who would dare to mess with something as classic as traditional chocolate chip cookies? For one, how much better can they really get? Any sane person would respond, "Not much." So we pull out all the stops here and see if we can't just push chocolate chip cookies over the edge, into a new place altogether—into an alternate universe where grilling and smoke and chocolate and just a kiss of salt against sweet make up the sun, sky, earth, and roaming deliciousness. This is classic—you just need a portal to an alternate dimension to get there. That portal is your salt block.

1 (10 to 12-inch) square salt block, at least 1½ inches thick

1¼ cups all-purpose flour

¾ cup ground walnuts

½ teaspoon baking soda

¼ teaspoon strong smoked salt, like red alder or hickory

½ cup (1 stick) unsalted butter, cut into chunks and softened

1 cup packed light brown sugar

1 large or extra-large egg

1 teaspoon pure vanilla extract

5 ounces semisweet chocolate, cut into ¼-inch chunks (1 cup)

½ cup walnut pieces

½ teaspoon large smoked flake salt, like Halen Môn Gold

1 cup fruitwood wood chips (apple, cherry, etc.)

Half an hour before you are ready to start grilling, put the salt block on an unheated gas grill. Heat the grill to low, cover the grill, and warm the block for 10 minutes. Raise the heat to medium and wait another 20 minutes. A laser thermometer aimed at the center of the block should register around 350°F. Turn the heat down to medium-low. If using charcoal, bank a chimney of red-hot charcoal briquettes to one side of the firebox. Put the block on the grill grate away from the fire and cover the grill. In 30 minutes, your block will be 350°F and ready for grilling.

While the salt block is heating, mix the flour, ground walnuts, baking soda, and salt in a small bowl. Set aside.

Mix the butter and brown sugar in a large bowl by hand with a wooden spoon or with an electric mixer using the paddle attachment until creamy. Mix in the egg and vanilla. Mix in the dry ingredients just until a cohesive dough forms. Mix in the chocolate and walnut pieces.

Line a small sheet pan or plate with foil. Divide the dough into 8 equal portions about ⅓ cup each. Wet your hands with cold water and form each piece of dough into a ball. Put on the foil. Flatten into ½-inch-thick disks. Sprinkle with flake salt.

CONTINUED

Put the wood chips on a sheet of foil.

Put the foil with the wood chips under the grill grate directly on the fire.

Transfer the cookies to the hot salt block. You should be able to fit all 8 on the block without crowding.

Close the grill lid and bake until set, browned on the bottom, dry on the top, but still moist inside and soft, 12 to 14 minutes. Remove with a spatula to a cooling rack and cool for at least 10 minutes before devouring.

A DOZEN PIZZAS
GRILLED ON A SALT BLOCK

Pizza is the ultimate template for ingredients: fresh, favorite, or far-flung. Just about any sauce will provide a base, just about any topping will elevate it, and just about any herbs and spices will tune the flavor to perfection. But what really sets everything on fire (figuratively speaking) is the dough sizzling and bubbling on the wicked hot salt block. The block protects the pizza from the direct heat of the grill, and at the same time puts an enormous amount of energy into the dough to cook it evenly and crisp. I prefer charcoal because it gets hotter and adds a bit more flavor, but a gas grill works great, too. For whole-wheat dough, see page 168.

2 (8 to 10-inch) square salt blocks, at least 1½ inches thick

PIZZA DOUGH (MAKES 2 MEDIUM OR 4 INDIVIDUAL PIZZAS)

1 cup warm water (110°F to 115°F)

2 teaspoons active dry yeast

1 teaspoon sugar

4 tablespoons extra-virgin olive oil, divided

2 teaspoons sea salt

2¾ cups bread flour, plus more as needed

Mild-tasting oil, for coating

2 tablespoons flavorful oil (see table, page 166)

½ cup sauce (see table)

1 cup shredded or crumbled cheese (see table)

About 3 cups toppings (see table)

Garnish (see table)

To prepare the dough, combine the water, yeast, and sugar in a large bowl, stirring until mixed. Let sit until foamy, about 5 minutes. Stir in 3 tablespoons of the olive oil, the salt, and flour and stir into a kneadable dough.

Turn onto a floured surface and knead until the dough is smooth and elastic, about 5 minutes. Add more flour as needed to keep the dough from sticking to your hands or the work surface, but try to add as little flour as possible.

Coat a large bowl with the remaining tablespoon of olive oil and add the dough, turning to coat it with the oil. Cover and let rise in a warm spot until doubled in bulk, about 1 hour, or overnight in the refrigerator.

An hour before you are ready to start grilling, put the salt blocks on an unheated gas grill. Heat the grill to low, cover the grill, and warm the block for 20 minutes. Raise the heat to medium and wait another 20 minutes. Raise it to high and wait another 20 minutes. A laser thermometer aimed at the center of the block should register around 550°F. If using charcoal, bank a chimney of red-hot charcoal briquettes to one side of the firebox. Put the block on the grill grate away from the fire and cover the grill. In 20 minutes, add a dozen more pieces of

CONTINUED

charcoal to the fire and, using grill gloves, move the block so that it is over the new coals. In 30 minutes, your block will be 550°F and ready for grilling.

While the salt block is heating, get your sauce and toppings together.

Cut 2 or 4 pieces of foil, depending on whether you are making 2 medium pizzas or 4 individual pizzas. Coat one of the pieces with mild oil. Divide the dough into 2 or 4 pieces. Put one piece of dough on the prepared foil and cover the other piece(s). Press and stretch the dough on the foil into a circle ⅛ to ¼ inch thick. Don't bother making a rim around the edge of the crust unless you like it for aesthetics. Coat the top of the dough round with mild oil. Repeat with the remaining dough and foil, oiling each dough round well and stacking them up.

Invert a circle of dough onto each salt block. If you can fit 2 pieces per stone, do so. Cover the grill and cook each round until bubbly on the top and lightly browned on the bottom, about 2 minutes. Invert the dough rounds so that the cooked side is up. Drizzle with a little of the flavorful oil. Spread the sauce over the top, leaving a rim all around. Scatter the cheese over the sauce and arrange the toppings over the cheese. Close the grill lid and grill until the cheese melts and the bottom is browned, about 6 minutes more. Remove to a cutting board.

Drizzle the pizzas with the remaining flavorful oil and top with the garnish.

Cut medium pizzas into 6 to 8 wedges; cut individual pizzas into quarters and serve.

CONTINUED

PIZZA TABLE

Here is a template for making twelve distinctive pizzas on a salt block. Follow the method in the recipe for A Dozen Pizzas Grilled on a Salt Block (page 163), substituting the ingredients listed in the table below.

PIZZA	OIL (2 TABLESPOONS)	SAUCE (½ CUP)	CHEESE (1 CUP)	TOPPINGS (ABOUT 3 CUPS)	GARNISH
Tijuana Caesar	Extra-virgin olive	Caesar dressing	Shaved Cotija	4 marinated anchovies, minced 8 shelled clams 8 shelled mussels 2 cloves garlic, sliced ½ red onion, thinly sliced ½ cup chopped ripe tomato 2 tablespoons chopped fresh cilantro, or cilantro pesto	2 cups coarsely chopped romaine More Caesar dressing, to taste
Asparagus and Chèvre	Grape seed	Lemon vinaigrette	Crumbled goat	2 cups shaved asparagus 1 cup grilled corn kernels 12 chives, sliced	2 fried eggs Big pinch fleur de sel 8 grilled thin lemon wedges
Broccoli Rabe, Porchetta, and Pecorino	Olive	Puttanesca	Burrata, grated Pecorino Romano	2 cups sautéed broccoli rabe 2 tablespoons roasted garlic ½ cup diced roasted peppers ½ cup diced porchetta or coppa ham ¼ cup golden raisins	Toasted pine nuts
Fig and Gorgonzola	Extra-virgin olive	Marinara	¾ cup shredded mozzarella ¼ cup crumbled Gorgonzola	8 ounces thinly sliced prosciutto, cut into strips 2 cups sliced fresh figs	1 cup watercress leaves Big pinch flake salt
Brussels and Pancetta	Extra-virgin olive	Pork ragù	8 ounces sliced buffalo milk mozzarella ¼ cup grated pecorino	2 tablespoons roasted garlic 4 ounces thinly sliced pancetta, sautéed and cut into strips 2 cups brussels sprout leaves	2 tablespoons coarsely chopped fresh rosemary leaves
X-X-Xochitl	Corn	Mole	Monterey Jack	2 cups pulled pork ½ cup thinly sliced yellow onion ½ cup drained canned black beans ½ cup grilled-corn kernels ¼ teaspoon minced habanero chile 1 or 2 serrano chiles, thinly sliced	¼ cup sliced black olives ¼ cup sour cream ⅓ cup guacamole 2 tablespoons chopped fresh cilantro

PIZZA	OIL (2 TABLESPOONS)	SAUCE (½ CUP)	CHEESE (1 CUP)	TOPPINGS (ABOUT 3 CUPS)	GARNISH
Wake Up and Smell the Bacon Breakfast Pizza	Extra-virgin olive	Barbecue	Equal parts smoked mozzarella and pepper Jack	4 slices crisp bacon, crumbled 2 ounces capicola, finely chopped 2 ounces sweet or hot soppressata, finely chopped ½ medium red onion, thinly sliced 1 cup chopped ripe tomato	2 fried eggs Big pinch fleur de sel Hot sauce, to taste
White Prosciutto and Liguria Olives	Extra-virgin olive	Alfredo	¾ cup shredded smoked mozzarella ¼ cup whole-milk ricotta	4 ounces thinly sliced prosciutto, cut into strips 2 tablespoons roasted garlic 2 cups sliced cremini mushrooms	1 cup chopped oil-cured Liguria olives 2 tablespoons chopped fresh flat-leaf parsley
Grilled Veggie Pesto	Extra-virgin olive	Pesto cream sauce	Mozzarella	8 grilled Asian eggplant slices 1 roasted red bell pepper, cut into strips 1 sliced medium red onion, grilled ¼ cup diced oil-cured sun-dried tomatoes 4 ounces cremini mushrooms, grilled and quartered	½ cup julienned fresh basil leaves 3 tablespoons grated Parmesan Big pinch flake salt
Savage Greens	Pine needle or other flavorful oil	Roasted mushroom gravy	Young Pecorino Toscano	6 trimmed ramps, grilled 3 cups fresh young greens, such as arugula, dandelion, kale, green garlic, etc. 4 ounces sliced wild mushrooms ¼ cup dried currants	2 tablespoons chopped blanched pine needles
4 Cheese 4 Sausage	Extra-virgin olive	Marinara	½ cup shredded mozzarella ¼ cup chopped Manchego 2 tablespoons grated Parmesan ¼ cup chopped aged Gouda	3 ounces each cooked, crumbled fennel sausage and cooked, sliced cotechino 2 ounces each Spanish chorizo, chopped, and sliced Merguez ½ cup thin shallot slices 2 garlic cloves, slivered	Fresh rosemary and flat-leaf parsley
Mascarpone and Strawberry	Almond	¼ cup mascarpone pureed with 6 strawberries, 1 tablespoon sugar, and ⅛ teaspoon ground cinnamon	½ cup mascarpone mixed with 5 ounces crumbled fresh chèvre	12 strawberries, hulled and sliced ½ cup fresh raspberries 1 cup fresh blueberries 1 tablespoon finely grated lime zest	¼ cup balsamic reduction 2 tablespoons chopped fresh mint leaves

MAKES ENOUGH FOR 2 MEDIUM OR 4 INDIVIDUAL PIZZAS
WHOLE-WHEAT PIZZA DOUGH

1 cup warm water (110°F to 115°F)

2 teaspoons active dry yeast

1 teaspoon sugar

4 tablespoons extra-virgin olive oil, divided

2 teaspoons kosher salt

1¼ cups whole-wheat flour

1½ cups bread flour, plus more as needed

Combine the water, yeast, and sugar in a large bowl, stirring until mixed. Let sit until foamy, about 5 minutes. Stir in 3 tablespoons of the oil, salt, and flours and stir into a kneadable dough.

Turn onto a floured surface and knead until the dough is smooth and elastic, about 5 minutes. Add more flour as needed to keep the dough from sticking to your hands or the work surface, but try to add as little flour as possible. Coat a large bowl with the remaining tablespoon of oil and add the dough, turning to coat it with the oil. Cover and let rise in a warm spot until doubled in bulk, about 1 hour, or overnight in the refrigerator. Proceed with assembling your pizzas as directed on page 166.

SALT BLOCK AREPAS WITH MEMBRILLO AND JAMÓN

Traveling just about anywhere south of the Texas border and north of Tierra del Fuego, you will find hot steel griddles, hot earthenware ovens, or hot stones with corn griddle cakes sizzling just shy of a char, awaiting the next meal. Everywhere you go, the griddle cakes are remarkably different. Arepas, the griddle-baked cornbread of Venezuela, are eaten for breakfast, lunch, dinner, and in between, stuffed with anything from queso blanco to roast turkey. Arepas are an ideal candidate for salt block grilling. Because the dough is so moist, the arepas pick up just enough salt to give the goodies stuffed inside a flavor bump that will have you rethinking everything from tortillas to johnnycakes.

1 (10-inch) square salt block, at least 1½ inches thick

2 cups hot tap water, about 120°F

½ teaspoon fleur de sel

2 tablespoons corn oil, plus more for coating

1½ cups arepa corn flour, white or yellow, such as Harina P.A.N.

½ cup membrillo (quince) paste

2 tablespoons orange juice

12 thin slices Ibérico or serrano ham

3 ounces Manchego or Ibérico cheese, thinly sliced

CONTINUED

Half an hour before you are ready to start grilling, put the salt block on an unheated gas grill. Heat the grill to low, cover the grill, and warm the block for 10 minutes. Raise the heat to medium and wait another 20 minutes. A laser thermometer aimed at the center of the block should register around 400°F. Turn the heat down to medium. If using charcoal, bank a chimney of red-hot charcoal briquettes to one side of the firebox. Put the block on the grill grate away from the fire and cover the grill. In 25 minutes, using grill gloves, move the blocks so that they are over the coals. In 5 minutes, your blocks will be 400°F and ready for grilling. Using grill gloves, move the blocks to the cooler side of the grill.

While the salt block is heating, mix the hot water, salt, and 2 tablespoons corn oil in a bowl. Slowly sprinkle in the arepa flour, stirring constantly to form a dough. Cover with a damp towel and set aside for 10 minutes to let the dough thicken. Divide into 12 portions and roll each into a ball. Working with one at a time, pat each into a 3-inch disk, about ½ inch thick. Coat each generously with corn oil.

Cook the arepas on the hot salt block until set, about 3 minutes per side. Move to the grill grate directly over the fire and cook until crunchy and grill-marked on the outside, 2 to 3 minutes per side.

While the arepas are cooking, mix the membrillo and orange juice into a jellylike consistency.

Slice the arepas open horizontally without going all the way through and spread the interior of each with 2 teaspoons of the membrillo mixture. Fold over the slices of ham and cheese and put them into the arepas. Serve while warm.

SALT-BLOCK-BAKED SMOKED-CHEESE SCONES WITH CHIPOTLE HONEY

Scones are narcissistic biscuits. They just think they're better—richer (due to added cream and yolks), more creative (blame the penchant for gilding scones with everything from cherries to chipotles), and more distinctive (biscuits are so damned circular). They are also built for salt block grilling because they are hard to mess up. One of my favorite grilling and baking recipes was the Salt-Baked Walnut Brioche Scones in my first salt block book, *Salt Block Cooking*. They contained just enough sugar to create a spectacular salted-caramel effect on the bottom of the scones. Here, we take a more savory path, with the bubbling cheese and charring scallion to show off yet another reason why scones are so good on a salt bock. Just because scones are narcissists doesn't mean they aren't special.

1 (10 to 12-inch) square salt block, at least 1½ inches thick

2 cups all-purpose flour

2 teaspoons baking powder

Pinch fine Himalayan salt

6 tablespoons unsalted butter, cut in 12 pieces

1 cup (4 ounces) shredded smoked Gouda, smoked cheddar, or smoked Jack cheese

3 scallions (green and white parts), trimmed and finely chopped

4 large egg yolks

¼ cup heavy cream

1 tablespoon spicy brown mustard

¼ cup honey

1 tablespoon chipotle hot pepper sauce

Unsalted butter, for serving

Half an hour before you are ready to start grilling, put the salt block on an unheated gas grill. Heat the grill to low, cover the grill, and warm the block for 10 minutes. Raise the heat to medium and wait another 20 minutes. A laser thermometer aimed at the center of the block should register around 400°F. Turn the heat down to medium. If using charcoal, bank a chimney of red-hot charcoal briquettes to one side of the firebox. Put the block on the grill grate away from the fire and cover the grill. In 25 minutes, using grill gloves, move the blocks so that they are over the coals. In 5 minutes, your blocks will be 400°F and ready for grilling. Using grill gloves, move the blocks to the cooler side of the grill.

While the salt block is heating, in the work bowl of a food processor equipped with a steel blade, combine the flour, baking powder, and salt. Process in pulses to combine.

Add the butter and process in 2 or 3 pulses until it is dispersed evenly. Add the cheese and scallions, and pulse 2 or 3 times, just long enough to mix in. Add the egg yolks, cream, and mustard and process until the mixture becomes a cohesive dough, about 40 seconds.

Turn the dough out onto a clean cutting board and pat into a 9-inch circle, about ¾ inch thick. Cut into 8 wedges.

Put the cut scones on the hot salt block, close the grill, and bake until puffed and browned, about 18 minutes.

While the scones are baking, mix the honey and hot sauce in a ramekin.

Remove the scones from the salt block and cool on a rack for 5 minutes before serving. Serve with the hot pepper–honey and butter.

ACKNOWLEDGMENTS

"Life is a journey, not a destination." Emerson's quote applies to the things that make up life as well. Writing is not a finished book, it is time spent—often alone, but often with people. It's these people who inspire me to write. My friend Andy Schloss gives me an opportunity time and again to learn more about food in a week than I otherwise might in a year—and to learn more about writing a book than I would otherwise learn in a lifetime. Working with my beloved editor Jean Lucas, art director Tim Lynch, designer Holly Swayne, photographer Aubrie LeGault, badass Jason French, stylist Ashley Marti, and intrepid publisher Kirsty Melville is an honor that expands my life's passions. The faith put in me by Taylor Klobertanz, Amy Newton, Abe Friedman, Mark Chapman, and the rest of the crew every time I tackle a book is as sure and miraculous as the Oregon rain, and it drives me to strive to be worthy of them as a colleague and employer. The generosity of Collin, Shannon, Delilah, Gabe, Peter, and Ben is a reward in a different way, a debt of gratitude that I hope to repay in regular installments of silvery I Am Love cocktails. The self-sacrifice, weird disco moves, and editorial acumen accorded me by my love, Kaitlin Hansen, is an anesthesia to the tribulations of writing and an amplifier of the exhilaration. Every once in a while, I glimpse a fleeting pride in my books from my discerning, laughing, yet inscrutable son Austin and my wily, wry, terminally precocious son Hugo, and these moments inspire me again and again to live up to be the father and friend they deserve. I'm thankful that exploring this book's sometimes kookily ethnic recipes gave me occasion to reflect on my affection for my ex-wife, Jennifer, though I never share this with her in person. Lastly, I am grateful to this book for providing me an opportunity to note my indelible love and admiration for my sister, Jenny—and so it is to her that I dedicate this book.

METRIC CONVERSIONS AND EQUIVALENTS

APPROXIMATE METRIC EQUIVALENTS

Volume

¼ teaspoon	1 milliliter
½ teaspoon	2.5 milliliters
¾ teaspoon	4 milliliters
1 teaspoon	5 milliliters
1¼ teaspoons	6 milliliters
1½ teaspoons	7.5 milliliters
1¾ teaspoons	8.5 milliliters
2 teaspoons	10 milliliters
1 tablespoon (½ fluid ounce)	15 milliliters
2 tablespoons (1 fluid ounce)	30 milliliters
¼ cup	60 milliliters
⅓ cup	80 milliliters
½ cup (4 fluid ounces)	120 milliliters
⅔ cup	160 milliliters
¾ cup	180 milliliters
1 cup (8 fluid ounces)	240 milliliters
1¼ cups	300 milliliters
1½ cups (12 fluid ounces)	360 milliliters
1⅔ cups	400 milliliters
2 cups (1 pint)	460 milliliters
3 cups	700 milliliters
4 cups (1 quart)	.95 liter
1 quart plus ¼ cup	1 liter
4 quarts (1 gallon)	3.8 liters

Weight

¼ ounce	7 grams
½ ounce	14 grams
¾ ounce	21 grams
1 ounce	28 grams
1¼ ounces	35 grams
1½ ounces	42.5 grams
1⅔ ounces	45 grams
2 ounces	57 grams
3 ounces	85 grams
4 ounces (¼ pound)	113 grams
5 ounces	142 grams
6 ounces	170 grams
7 ounces	198 grams
8 ounces (½ pound)	227 grams
16 ounces (1 pound)	454 grams
35.25 ounces (2.2 pounds)	1 kilogram

Length

⅛ inch	3 millimeters
¼ inch	6 millimeters
½ inch	1¼ centimeters
1 inch	2½ centimeters
2 inches	5 centimeters
2½ inches	6 centimeters
4 inches	10 centimeters
5 inches	13 centimeters
6 inches	15¼ centimeters
12 inches (1 foot)	30 centimeters

METRIC CONVERSION FORMULAS

To Convert	Multiply
Ounces to grams	Ounces by 28.35
Pounds to kilograms	Pounds by .454
Teaspoons to milliliters	Teaspoons by 4.93
Tablespoons to milliliters	Tablespoons by 14.79
Fluid ounces to milliliters	Fluid ounces by 29.57
Cups to milliliters	Cups by 236.59
Cups to liters	Cups by .236
Pints to liters	Pints by .473
Quarts to liters	Quarts by .946
Gallons to liters	Gallons by 3.785
Inches to centimeters	Inches by 2.54

OVEN TEMPERATURES

To convert Fahrenheit to Celsius, subtract 32 from Fahrenheit, multiply the result by 5, then divide by 9.

Description	Fahrenheit	Celsius	British Gas Mark
Very cool	200°	95°	0
Very cool	225°	110°	¼
Very cool	250°	120°	½
Cool	275°	135°	1
Cool	300°	150°	2
Warm	325°	165°	3
Moderate	350°	175°	4
Moderately hot	375°	190°	5
Fairly hot	400°	200°	6
Hot	425°	220°	7
Very hot	450°	230°	8
Very hot	475°	245°	9

COMMON INGREDIENTS AND THEIR APPROXIMATE EQUIVALENTS

1 cup uncooked white rice = 185 grams
1 cup all-purpose flour = 125 grams
1 stick butter (4 ounces • ½ cup • 8 tablespoons) = 115 grams
1 cup butter (8 ounces • 2 sticks • 16 tablespoons) = 225 grams
1 cup brown sugar, firmly packed = 220 grams
1 cup granulated sugar = 200 grams

Information compiled from a variety of sources, including *Recipes into Type* by Joan Whitman and Dolores Simon (Newton, MA: Biscuit Books, 1993); *The New Food Lover's Companion* by Sharon Tyler Herbst (Hauppauge, NY: Barron's, 2013); and *Rosemary Brown's Big Kitchen Instruction Book* (Kansas City, MO: Andrews McMeel, 1998).

INDEX

SALT BLOCK GRILLING

Andrews McMeel Publishing
a division of Andrews McMeel Universal
1130 Walnut Street, Kansas City, Missouri 64106

www.andrewsmcmeel.com

As when using anything at high temperature, cooking
on salt blocks poses risks. If you wish to cook on a
salt block, proceed at your own discretion with caution.
Neither the author nor the publisher assumes any
responsibility for damages, injury, or loss due to the
heating of Himalayan salt products.

17 18 19 20 21 SDB 10 9 8 7 6 5 4 3 2 1

ISBN: 978-1-4494-8315-9

Library of Congress Control Number: 2016949277

Editor: Jean Z. Lucas
Designer: Holly Swayne
Art Director: Tim Lynch
Production Editor: Maureen Sullivan
Production Manager: Carol Coe
Photographer: Aubrie LeGault
Food Stylist/Prop Stylist: Ashley Marti

Photo credits: Mark Bitterman, pages v, 2, 8–9, 11,
12, 23, 24, 25, 105

ATTENTION: SCHOOLS AND BUSINESSES

Andrews McMeel books are available at quantity discounts
with bulk purchase for educational, business, or sales
promotional use. For information, please e-mail the
Andrews McMeel Publishing Special Sales Department:
specialsales@amuniversal.com.